FRANÇOISE PIALOUX

IBIZA
LAND AND SEA

100 Sun-Drenched Recipes

EDITING AND STYLING:
FRANÇOISE LEFÉBURE
PHOTOGRAPHS:
ALBERT FONT

ABRAMS I NEW YORK

CONTENTS

Ibiza. A bright summer morning at the *Terrasses*. Mimine's *finca*, signposted on Santa Eulalia Road by a large rock daubed in Klein blue, is beginning to stir in the dewy coolness. Its white walls stretch, breathing in the delicious country air. The old well and the white-washed facade have not yet been dazzled by the glare that will soon engulf them, spattering them with shadows and drops of sunshine. A delicate Madonna-blue ribbon of shadow rolls like a wave below the eaves until it mingles with the limpid blue of the sky.

This Ibiza blue, reputed to keep insects at bay, is the light blue *azul ultramar* of washing, and is the colour that draws us all to the island. A few wingbeats away, palm trees, Barbary fig plants, pomegranate trees, cannas, bamboos, agaves and olive trees gently wave their branches like paintbrushes dipped in brilliant green, sketching in the landscape. The birds are singing loudly, three geckos peep over the threshold of their drystone hiding place and the two pools mirror a passing cloud. A true Garden of Eden…

Zia, the house dog, is, as always, dozing beneath one of the terrace tables. The hotel guests are still asleep, scattered among the various comfortable rooms. Guests are easy to recognise — they drift about with the dazed, happy expressions of epicurean travellers having fallen upon their dream holiday location. There's no rush. Yesterday, it was Tuesday — Couscous Day.

The couscous dinner is a regular date that people mark with three crosses on the *Ibicenca* calendar, knowing that everyone will be there — the friends from the other side of the island, the usuals, the new people, the pretty tanned *guapas*, the loyal fans, the ageing hippies, the old sea salts, the children, the lovers, the "in" people, the tourists in shorts, the incognito stars and the epicureans — all anxious to share in the ritual of a rare

privilege and a joyous meal under the stars. After the laughing and greeting and feasting on the rolled, spun, thrown, endlessly aired couscous grains so light that they float, the *finca* tidies away its pots and pans and returns to the calm of early morning.

But don't worry — in the odd-looking pistachio-yellow kitchen as busy as a market bazaar, clanging with hanging spoons and piled-up frying pans, and as appetising as a chocolate madeleine, the bread has already been baked. The seasonal fruit juices, brimful of vitamins, have already been squeezed and the divine home-made orange and lemon marmalade has already been spooned into bowls and pots, crammed with Ibiza sunshine and, above all, the love of a single woman. That woman is Françoise Pialoux.

But nearly everyone has always called her Mimine.

Mimine is not a cook like anyone else. Mimine is a character who loves life — she's generous, gay, talkative. There's no messing about with Mimine — she's energetic, gathering people around her, and she enjoys simple tastes, only proper food. She looks after you, a spontaneous manager with a huge heart, whose *finca* would not be what it is without her, and her hotel certainly not this *Terrasses*. In fact, if you listen carefully to the music of the *Terrasses*, you will observe that the *finca* only really wakes up in the morning when Mimine's laugh or lively voice rings out as she bursts into the kitchen, radiant, her apron crooked, hair pinned back anyhow, a bunch of fresh mint from the vegetable garden ready to plonk on the table, or a bunch of cosmos clutched in one hand and an armful of organic vegetables she's chosen for a lunch that can last all day.

So there you have it — the heart of the *Terrasses* is Mimine!

How on earth can someone from the French mainland have settled here, rooted even more than locals in the deep red soil of the *payés* (peasant) fields, and anchored in the shallow waters of an island shore? How is it possible that a little mop-haired girl born in the 14th district of Paris could fall in love with herbs, spices, aubergines, octopus, red mullet, citrus fruit, figs and chocolate, to the point of instantly inventing tons of delicious ways of serving them, as easily as she can pronounce her enthusiastic *"¿Holà que tal?"* greeting every morning?

Well, before she was even six, Françoise would spend six months of the year in Liamontou, Aveyron, with *"Mémé Combettes"* and Marcel. From Easter to Halloween, she breathed the pure air of her paternal grandparents' small rural village. There's nothing like the country air for a growing child… Françoise attended the village school, gathered linden blossoms, brought in the wood, picked huge bunches of flowers for the church and washed the old-fashioned way — in a big tub in front of the fire. Sylvie, her grandma, was a good cook and often invited guests. The granite house with its stone roof was always full, the silver cutlery always out. No one was better than *"Mémé Combettes"* at preparing stuffed vegetables, *fouace* (local

breads) or milk curd cakes, even though these traditional dishes were not enough to fatten up little Françoise, too skinny in her grandma's view.

Back in the Paris region, Françoise would attend the convent school at Fontenay-aux-Roses, where she lived with her family. There, Henri and Marie, her maternal grandparents, had started a hotel and restaurant in 1949, after leaving their hamlet of Albusquiès near Rodez. Already, at eight, the little girl was a live wire. Even if there was homework, no sooner had she left the school gates than she was at the stove in the Café de la Gare, where Marie might be preparing a *choucroute* or a Veal Marengo or perching the last choux pastry ball full of luscious cream on the top of a cake ready for a wedding organised in the family restaurant. Little Françoise hung around, helped where she could, devouring all the cooking tricks with her big eyes, as curious as the cat, drinking in the scents and nourishing her heart. Even as an adolescent, a weekly boarder at her school, Notre-Dame des Oiseaux, she would find her way to Marie's kitchen in Fontenay-aux-Roses at the weekend. Mimine probably already knew how to be a fantastic cook even without really learning or realising she was.

Mimine married before she was twenty, and with Michel she departed for Algeria, where he had been appointed as a law professor at Oran University. Françoise would have been happy to live there the rest of her life. She discovered food that she had never known before and fell under the spells woven by a thousand and one spicy scents. Naturally, that was where she learned how to roll couscous. But this first introduction only lasted two years — an appetiser. Back to Paris they came — she, Michel and baby Cyprien — with luggage they didn't want to unpack and the overwhelming desire to find somewhere they could build themselves a home.

Luck and the favourable winds of the Mediterranean played into their hands in September 1977, when they embarked on a sailing boat at Cassis, bound for Alicante. Michel, in his hippy phase, worked as a ship hand and Mimine, as the ship's cook. Overcome by seasickness, she disembarked at Ibiza and filled her first *Ibicenco* shopping basket with local produce from the market in the old town. The spell was cast. Opening wide eyes in search of freedom, she succumbed to the charm of the white streets, met young hippies living the bohemian life, and still remembers to this day the nonchalant, graceful Swede wearing trousers with one stripey leg and one leg dotted with stars. She vowed to return. And return she did, with her parents in May 1978, and then again, and yet again in 1980, the year she discovered her famous *finca* (which would later become her hotel) that she rented for the holidays, and even began to rebuild, since it was virtually falling down. Meanwhile, with Frédérique, who would later be her mainstay at the *Terrasses*, she managed a restaurant near Cala Tarida for the holiday season, and began serious cooking.

The true, once-and-for-all move to Ibiza was in 1985. When her second son was born and Michel was starting at his Paris law firm, Françoise defied convention and decided to set up permanently on the mythical island where anxieties flew out of the window. Little Rafou (Rafael was his real name) was to grow up lulled by the tolerance and hedonism of the *Isla Blanca*!

Obviously, all the holiday trips had required somewhere to stay, and now Françoise needed a place to set up, at least for her first attempt at a business. But she trusted her luck, and the old ruin she had rented in 1980 was going to be that place.

"That old *finca* was made for me — that's just how it was!"

The old abandoned house on the eastern side of the island, reached by the country roads and located just before Santa Eularia del Rio, was a gift from God, her "farm palace", that would need entire rebuilding, but that was fine. "We lived the hippy life. Nobody had a telephone — you had to go to the Hotel Montessol in town to get news every day. We were carefree." Even during the building works, there was always a big improvised meal, fun and laughter, the pattering bare feet of kids toasted in the sun like warm bread, and tents and dens that Mimine would build them with bits of sheet and her own memories of treehouses and wooden castles made by her father.

And so, *poc a poc*, as Françoise always says, she reinvented space, created new ones, intuitively planted a previously inexistent garden, and enlarged the old farm. Little by little, with a bungalow here, another there, the way you'd add rooms on for friends in an old family home. Just to be able to give them all a bed, have them round her table and enjoy simple pleasures together.

The *Terrasses* was born. In June 1988, Jane Birkin became Françoise's first client. With her *boca a boca* and *poc a poc*, Françoise managed to gather around her a tribe of artists, photographers, laid-back holidaymakers, people who wanted the simple life and enjoyed real, good cooking.

Why was she so successful? Because Mimine was at the stove making delicious food all day long, just as, before her, her grandmother Marie had done, and she had the art of making her hotel into a home, just as her mother Henriette had done with the Café de la Gare. It runs through the family...

"I feel protected when I'm on my island."

Mimine knows her way around now and she is at home, free as the wind that blows from the land and drawn to the sea breezes. Ibiza is her island and the *Terrasses* is her island on the island. A sort of second family, where the omnipresence of women over the generations and life has forged the spirit of this place. From Mimine to Frédérique, from Aïcha to Hanane, Fatima, Sarah, Maria, Catalina, Martina, Karima and then Oriane, Chloé, Charline… all these women are part, or were part, of the *finca*, just like little pebbles that you collect to build a fine adventure. Of course, we must not forget the men loyal to the *Terrasses* — Bachir, Abdoul and others — or the fellow maestros of the kitchen — Roshan, Olivier and Juanito — who have been sensitive enough to Mimine's style of cooking to be able to adapt.

And what cooking! Light, authentic, spontaneous, ripened in the Balearic sun and crammed full of memories of travels. Her passion for herbs, coriander and parsley? That came from Vietnam. Tajines and couscous? Memories of Algeria. The spices? Morocco, of course. As for the aubergines, or the lemons she adores, they appear to have come to Mimine from Nature itself, and the red soil that forms the fields in the interior of the island. A rich soil that gives the extraordinary flavour to the potatoes and vegetables and inspires Mimine to invent recipes using organic products and use permaculture techniques in her vegetable garden and orchard. But they are not the only inspiration. "What is more delicious than a basket of figs picked straight from those extraordinary trees that stand like old parasols in the fields, their heavy branches firmly supported by a crow's nest of sticks and poles? They dominate the landscape at Formentera, the neighbouring island that we can reach in a short boat ride for a day trip." She will also tell you stories of how beautiful winter walks are when the almond trees are in flower in Santa Agnès Valley, and how after eating a good tortilla at Can Cosmi, the village bar and grocer's just by the church, she can walk down the path to her beach cabin at Cala Salada. Because of course Mimine found herself a second home, a small secret paradise on the seashore, looking like a boat floating on the water.

"From my fisherman's cabin it's as if I were drinking in the Mediterranean."

There, their table facing the horizon, watching her grandchildren Clara, Alice and Théo running along the shore, she and her friends can drink in the Ibiza by the sea that Mimine is deeply attached to. Not for her the magnificent white sand of the overcrowded summer beaches: "I much prefer the hidden coves in the north of the island, the boathouses made of driftwood, the gentle water frilling along the old wooden posts where the fishing boats slip in, and where you can feast on the day's catch of sea bream or squid, breathe in the salty air and cook up a huge pan of *arroz a banda* to share in the fisherman's cabin." So — Ibiza *payés*, or Ibiza *pescado*? Mimine can't decide… and in fact, refuses to choose, in her *Terrasses* kitchen. She mingles a little of both, tops them with a skilful ladleful of good humour, and our meal suddenly acquires the flavour of the land… or of the sea… or perhaps both! Welcome to Ibiza!

TASTES OF
THE COUNTRYSIDE

Dishes from the vegetable garden

"We eat produce that is good for our health. I don't care whether vegetables are pretty or not. What matters is that they should be the healthiest and most natural possible. Herbs, salad leaves, artichokes, christophines, squash, avocados or rhubarb all come from my vegetable garden and orchard, that I am learning to cultivate using permaculture techniques. Failing that, I fill my baskets at the eco-bio *finca* on Santa Eularia Road or the one in Can Muson…"

A NICE HEALTHY SALAD

"I invented this salad for a yoga retreat I organised at the *Terrasses*. It is true that what with the grains, shoots and tender vegetables, it is a real booster. I often accompany it with a glass of green gazpacho, a tasty little soup made of avocado and cucumber."

Precook the lentils *al dente* in a pan of unsalted cold water for 25 minutes over a medium flame. Cook the quinoa for 15 minutes in unsalted cold water. If you are using a rice cooker, put in one measure of quinoa to 1½ measures of water. Drain well and allow to cool at room temperature.

Blanch the asparagus and mange-tout peas successively in a pan of water salted with coarse salt and bicarbonate of soda. Drain and refrigerate.

To serve, mix all the ingredients — the lentils, quinoa, asparagus, mange-tout peas, rocket, peeled and sliced avocados and halved tomatoes. Top with pomegranate seeds, chopped shallots, finely sliced onion stems and herbs. Toss quickly and decorate with the seeds and chopped onion stems or basil as wished.

Serve this salad with a separate bowl of sauce prepared from all the ingredients. Thus the guests can choose how much sauce they want.

SERVES 6
Cooking time: 42 minutes

250 g (8 oz.) green lentils
250 g (8 oz.) quinoa
6 green asparagus spears
2 handfuls of mange-tout peas
½ tsp. bicarbonate of soda
1 handful of rocket leaves
2 avocados
12–16 cocktail tomatoes
1 pomegranate
2 shallots
A few spring onion shoots
A little coriander or parsley
Mixed seeds (sunflower, sesame, linseed, etc.) to decorate
Spring onion shoots or basil leaves (optional)

FOR THE SAUCE
1 tsp. sesame oil
1 tsp. balsamic vinegar
1 tsp. wine vinegar
(preferably Sherry vinegar)
3 tbsp. olive oil
Salt, pepper

AVOCADO **VITAMIN APPETISER**

"I usually serve this green gazpacho crammed with vitamins alongside my healthy salad, and I always use organic fruit and vegetables to whip it up in a trice."

SERVES 6
Preparation: chill for 1 hour before serving
No cooking

1 avocado
1 cucumber
2 spring onions
1 celery stick
1 handful of flat parsley
1 green apple
4 or 5 rocket leaves
Juice of one lemon
Olive oil
Salt, pepper
Mixed organic seeds such as linseed, sunflower, sesame, etc. (optional)
A few basil leaves

Peel and cube the vegetables, chop the parsley, apple and rocket, and put everything through the blender. Add a little cold water. Chill for 1 hour. Stir.

Just before serving, stir in the lemon juice, a slash of olive oil, and salt and pepper to taste.

Pour the gazpacho into bowls or verrines, decorate with mixed seeds and a few basil leaves. Drink this vitamin-loaded brew at any time of day or serve as a starter along with a salad.

HARIRA **MOROCCAN SOUP**

"This soup was a revelation for me. It was in Morocco, 40 years ago, and it was the first time I'd ever tasted coriander, too. In fact, it was such an explosion of flavours that I ordered another bowl straight-away! The original recipe has vegetables and lamb, but I like it just as much without meat."

SERVES 8
Cooking time: 35 minutes

3 carrots
2 turnips
2 celery sticks
1 courgette
1 aubergine
2 onions
3 cloves of garlic
2 tbsp. cumin
1 tbsp. crushed coriander seeds
½ tsp. nutmeg
800 g (1 lb. 12 oz.) approx. crushed, raw, peeled tomatoes
200 g (7 oz.) chickpeas (canned)
1 handful of parsley
1 bunch of coriander
Olive oil
Salt, pepper

Prepare all your vegetables: peel and cut the carrots and turnips into large cubes.

Cut the celery, courgette and aubergine into small pieces.

Then peel and slice the onions and garlic and fry in a pot over a hot flame with a little olive oil and the spices — the cumin, the coriander seeds and the nutmeg.

Now add the crushed tomatoes, all the cubed vegetables and the drained chickpeas. Season with salt and pepper, add the parsley, part of the fresh coriander and cover with water. Cook over a brisk flame for 30 minutes, then blend. Serve piping hot, sprinkled with the remainder of the chopped coriander.

OLIVIER'S **CARROT CROQUETTES**

"This recipe is simple, tasty and fun. Serve the croquettes crammed with vitamins for aperitifs or as an accompaniment to grilled meat or fish. It's the *Terrasses*'s cook's great idea for making kids eat carrots!"

SERVES 8

Preparation: 1 hour ahead
of time for the mix
Cooking time: 4–6 minutes
per batch

750 g (1 lb. 9 oz.) carrots
1 tbsp. olive oil
100 g (3½ oz.) plain flour
(T45 or T55)
Salt, pepper
Oil for the deep fryer

Peel and grate the carrots, then mix with the olive oil and flour. Season with salt and pepper, then leave to rest for one hour at room temperature.

Heat the oil to 170°C (340°F).

When the mixture is ready and you are almost ready to eat, shape balls about the size of a ping-pong ball, pressing hard to get the juice out, before dropping into the deep fryer. Make as many croquettes as possible, until no mix is left. Cook for 3–4 minutes, then drain on kitchen paper.

Do not overcook the croquettes. It is better to recook them for 2 minutes in even hotter oil (180°C [360°F]) at the last minute. Drain again and serve immediately.

SWISS CHARD TART WITH OLIVES

"For this recipe, I sometimes use my black olive shortcrust pastry, which makes it even tastier. And when I can't find good chard leaves, I do it with spinach leaves. It is delicious piping hot, but you can also eat it warm for a picnic."

Make the shortcrust pastry following our recipe on page 241. Immediately line a rectangular baking tin or a round one about 30 cm (12 in.) in diameter, and refrigerate for 1 hour. Note that you can also use the black olive shortcrust pastry recipe on page 240.

Rinse the chard leaves, cut them into small pieces and blanch in a pot of boiling water for three minutes.

Fry the sliced onions and chopped garlic in olive oil and then add the chard. Mix and cook over a hot flame for just a few seconds. Set aside.

In a bowl, mix the eggs, liquid cream and shredded thyme, adding a little pepper.

Remove the pastry shell in its tin from the fridge and spread the chard, onion and garlic mixture over the bottom. Pour the beaten egg mixture over the top and sprinkle with the grated Manchego or Parmesan. Bake for about 20 minutes at 170°C (340°F). Add the pitted olives on the top and return to the oven for 5 minutes.

Serve this hot chard tart for lunch with a nice green salad.

SERVES 8
Preparation: chill the pastry dough for one hour
Cooking time: 30 minutes

FOR THE SHORTCRUST PASTRY
(see recipe on page 241)
300 g (11 oz.) plain flour
(T45 or T55)
150 g (5½ oz.) butter
5–6 cl (3 tbsp.) water
2 pinches of salt

FOR THE FILLING
1 bunch of Swiss chard
2 onions
3 garlic cloves
3 organic eggs
4 tbsp. liquid double cream
½ tsp. thyme
A little pepper
100 g (3½ oz.) grated Manchego or Parmesan cheese
120 g (4 oz.) pitted black olives
Olive oil

OLIVIER'S RISOTTO WITH SMALL LOCAL ARTICHOKES

"I just love Ibiza's tiny artichokes… I plant them in my vegetable plot but I also buy them from the local organic food cooperative, Ecofeixes. When there are no artichokes, Olivier prepares this same delicious risotto with asparagus and scallops. He uses the asparagus stems, and three-quarters into the cooking time he adds the asparagus tips and the scallops."

SERVES 6

Cooking time: 25 minutes approx.

12 small local artichokes
3 shallots
1 clove of garlic
500 g (1 lb.) risotto or pudding rice
15 cl (9 tbsp.) white wine
1 l (2 pints) chicken stock (or vegetable stock for vegetarians)
1 tbsp. butter
1 tbsp. grated Parmesan
1 handful of chopped parsley
Olive oil
1 tsp. salt
3 turns of the pepper mill

Take off the artichoke leaves, remove hairy centre and cut into small strips.

Peel and finely chop the shallots. Peel and crush the garlic. Heat a little olive oil over a high flame and fry the artichokes for 2 minutes. Set aside.

Heat the oil in a sauté pan, add the shallots and crushed garlic and sweat for a few seconds. Then add the rice and heat over a low flame for 1–2 minutes until transparent.

Pour in the white wine and stir until the wine evaporates. Next, gradually add the stock at room temperature, stirring constantly and keeping an eye on the heat until the rice has absorbed all the stock. This should take about 20 minutes.

Add the artichokes, stir, and then incorporate the butter and grated Parmesan. Stir one more time and decorate with chopped parsley just before serving.

ARTICHOKE AND GARLIC STIR-FRY

"I first tasted this recipe one day near Alicante, in a restaurant lost in the middle of artichoke fields, where most of the menu consisted of artichokes, of course! The artichoke preparation is a bit fiddly, unfortunately, but it's worth it because this stir-fry starter is so delicious."

SERVES 6

Cooking time: 10 minutes

15 new, very tender artichokes
2 organic lemons
3 tbsp. olive oil
6 young garlic cloves
A few pinches of *fleur de sel*

Clean the artichokes thoroughly, take off the large green leaves, cut into two to remove the hairy chokes, then cut again, leaving only two centimetres of tender inner leaves. Finally, cut the hearts into two or four pieces. Place them in water containing the lemon cut into large pieces to stop the artichoke from blackening.

Now heat olive oil in a wok or deep pan over a hot flame, drop in the artichoke pieces and unpeeled garlic. Cook for 8–10 minutes, stirring constantly.

Just before the end of cooking, add the sea salt and allow it to dissolve for two seconds in the wok. Serve immediately as an appetiser or starter.

BLACK TOMATO TART

"This black and red tart is magnificent! Sometimes I replace the black olive shortcrust pastry by one coloured with black cuttlefish ink. I buy this, frozen or otherwise, and add it to the pastry in a small glass of water with a pinch of salt. If I do that, I add another 100 g of pitted black olives in the crostini mix. Finally, if it is for vegetarians, I don't add anchovies, and it is just as nice."

SERVES 8

Preparation: refrigerate pastry
for 1 hour
Cooking time: 50 minutes

A baking tin 30 cm (12 in.)
in diameter

FOR THE BLACK OLIVE SHORTCRUST PASTRY
(see recipe on page 240)
250 g (8 oz.) pitted black olives
125 g (4 oz.) butter
250 g (8 oz.) plain flour
(T45 or T55)

FOR THE FILLING
1.5 kg (3 lb.) plum tomatoes
(Roma)
250 g (8 oz.) mozzarella
70 g (2½ oz.) pitted black olives
20 g (2 tbsp.) capers
5 anchovies
2 pinches of pepper
5 basil leaves
1 drizzle of olive oil

Prepare the black olive shortcrust pastry following the recipe on page 240 and chill for 1 hour. Then roll out the pastry with very little flour so that it stays nice and black. Line a lightly buttered tin and bake blind for 20 minutes at 170°C (340°F).

Meanwhile, peel the tomatoes either with a peeling knife or by steaming and then dropping into iced water to loosen the skin. Now cut them in two and deseed without tearing them. Bake for 20 minutes at 150°C (320°F).

Prepare the crostini paste, blending the mozzarella, pitted olives, capers, anchovies, pepper and basil leaves in the food mixer.

Spread the crostini mixture on the bottom of the black olive pastry shell. Top with the halved tomatoes, drizzle with olive oil and return to the oven for 5–10 minutes. Serve nicely browned with a small salad of rocket or spinach leaves.

VIETNAMESE **PANCAKES**

"The first time I ate this pancake was in Hué, Vietnam. It really is a meal in itself! So I brought the idea back with me… especially as it's totally gluten and lactose free and can be adapted for vegetarians if you skip the pork."

SERVES 4
(4 PANCAKES)
Cooking time: 9–10 minutes

FOR THE BATTER
200 g (7 oz.) rice flour
(or wheat flour if preferred)
1 tsp. turmeric
2 pinches of salt
3 tsp. caster sugar
4 eggs
60 cl (2½ cups) coconut milk
60 cl (2½ cups) water
A little sunflower oil

FOR THE FILLING
80 g (2½ oz.) peas
80 g (2½ oz.) snow peas
(mange-tout peas)
4 green asparagus spears
4 field mushrooms
8 shrimps
160 g (5 oz.) minced pork
Stems of 8 spring onions
40 g (1½ oz.) bean sprouts
½ bunch of coriander
½ bunch of fresh mint
A little soya or nem sauce
Sunflower oil

First prepare the batter by combining the flour, turmeric, salt, sugar and beaten eggs and adding the coconut milk and water.

In a pan of boiling water, blanch the green vegetables: peas, mange-tout peas and asparagus. Drain and place in a bowl of iced water. Drain again and set aside at room temperature.

Fry the sliced mushrooms in a small oiled pan over a hot flame for one minute. Set aside at room temperature.

Peel the shrimps and sauté with the pork in a frying pan with a little sunflower oil. Divide all the ingredients (pork, shrimps, cooked vegetables) into four portions so it is easier to fill the pancakes.

At the last minute, just before serving, cook the pancakes. A pan measuring 24 cm (10 in.) is a good size. If you have two of the same, it will be easier and quicker to cook them, of course!

For each pancake, pour one ladle of batter into the pan, in which you have warmed a little sunflower oil over a medium flame. When the pancake has browned on one side, cover one half with the pork, shrimps and vegetables. Leave to cook one more minute. Then add the spring onion stems cut into small pieces, then the beansprouts and, as wished, the fresh herbs.

Fold the pancake in two when well-browned and slide onto a plate.

Drizzle with soya (or nem) sauce and serve immediately. You can accompany these pancakes by a small side salad.

AVOCADO **TARTARE**

"This is extremely quick to prepare, but the most important thing is to have good avocados! I serve this tartare with a few rocket leaves and a slice of crunchy toast. Sometimes I add little cubes of tofu to give energy to a vegetarian or even vegan dish."

SERVES 4

No cooking

2 avocados
2 tomatoes
I cucumber
2 spring onions
A few coriander leaves

FOR THE SAUCE
I tbsp. soya sauce
½ tsp. wasabi
2 tbsp. olive oil
Juice of I lime

Peel the avocados, tomatoes, cucumber and spring onions and cut everything into small cubes, including the spring onion stems. Prepare a sauce with the soya sauce, wasabi, olive oil and lime juice.

To serve, mix the vegetable cubes with the sauce and scatter with a few coriander leaves. Eat chilled and accompany with rocket leaves.

RATATOUILLE IN COURGETTE SUSHIS

"I improvised these sushis over twenty years ago for a buffet at a wedding. At the time, sushis weren't so fashionable and I wanted to make them more Mediterranean. Anyway, the groom was a vegetarian!"

SERVES 10
(3–4 sushis per person)
Cooking time: 17 minutes approx.

FOR THE SUSHIS
3 unpeeled courgettes
A few chives

FOR THE RATATOUILLE
1 large aubergine
2 tomatoes
½ green pepper
½ red pepper
1 onion
1 tbsp. pitted black olives
4–5 basil leaves
1 tbsp. olive oil
Salt, pepper

First prepare your ratatouille. Half-peel the aubergine and peel the other vegetables — tomatoes, peppers and onion — completely. Cut everything into small cubes.

Heat 1 tbsp. olive oil in a pan and sauté the vegetables with the chopped black olives and chopped basil leaves. Season, stir and leave to cook gently for about 15 minutes. The vegetables must remain crunchy. Allow to cool.

Next, prepare the courgette strips. Cut off the ends of the courgettes and slice lengthwise in ribbons about 2 mm (1/16 in.) thick from the main body. Blanch for one minute in a pot of salted boiling water, drain and leave to cool on a cloth.

Finally, build your sushis. Take a courgette strip, roll, and tie a chive stalk around it. Fill the ring with a spoonful of cold ratatouille. Repeat for each sushi. Refrigerate until serving and eat with fingers.

SUMMER **PRESSED TOMATOES**

"I find this really spectacular and I'm always anxious to get to July when the tomatoes are well ripened so that I can do this dish. The only problem is, it's difficult to slice, so I use an electric carver to get decent-looking slices."

SERVES 10–12

Preparation one day ahead
No cooking

2 kg (4 lb.) bright red plum
tomatoes (Roma)
100 g (3½ oz.) anchovies
3 drizzles of best-quality
olive oil
Pepper
A few basil leaves
(to decorate)
Fleur de sel to taste
A little tapenade (optional
accompaniment)

Peel the tomatoes, cut into four and remove seeds. Line a terrine dish (or oblong cake tin) with cling film and on the bottom place one layer of tomatoes, two or three lines of anchovies lengthwise along the tin, a little pepper and a drizzle of olive oil. Add a second layer of tomatoes, anchovy lines, pepper and the drizzle of olive oil. Finish filling the terrine dish with just a layer of tomatoes and a drizzle of olive oil.

Now place a rectangular plate or piece of wood on the terrine with a weight on top to press down on the tomatoes. Refrigerate for 24 hours. Be careful! Do not on any account put salt in this terrine, because the tomatoes will leak.

The next day, serve the terrine decorated with a few basil leaves and accompany with *fleur de sel* and a bowl of tapenade (see recipe on page 249).

"On Ibiza, it's magical! Squashes practically grow all by themselves in our soil! Right from the end of summer, we pick the pumpkins and squashes and store them carefully, and then, easy peasy, I cook them in either sweet or savoury dishes."

BREAKFAST **PUMPKIN CAKE**

"I like the idea of starting the day by eating a vegetable… So as soon as autumn sets in, I serve this simple cake for breakfast. It has that homespun flavour that I like…"

SERVES 6–8

Cooking time: 1 hour 10 minutes

A cake or baking tin 26–28 cm (11–12 in.) in diameter and 5 cm (2 in.) deep

500 g (1 lb.) pumpkin or butternut
180 g (6 oz.) softened butter
220 g (7½ oz.) caster sugar
6 egg yolks
1 full-fat yoghurt
220 g (7½ oz.) plain flour (T45)
2½ tsp. baking powder
1 tbsp. bicarbonate of soda
½ tsp. bergamot seeds
5 egg whites
1 pinch of salt

Peel and deseed the pumpkin or butternut and cut into large pieces. Place in an earthenware dish and bake at 170°C (340°F) for 30–40 minutes. Remove and mash the flesh with a fork. Weigh the mash before setting aside. There should be 400 g.

Beat the softened butter and the sugar in a bowl until white and fluffy. Add the egg yolks, beating constantly, then add the pumpkin or butternut, yoghurt, flour mixed with baking powder and bicarbonate, and the pinch of salt. Mix. Now whip the egg whites and delicately fold them into the pumpkin mix.

Pour into the greased cake tin lined with buttered greaseproof paper. Bake for 30 minutes at 165°C (330°F).

PUMPKIN SOUP WITH TURMERIC

"Because I plant lots of squash seeds in my vegetable plot, the harvest is always very abundant! So sometimes I hollow out little butternuts to make soup bowls — they are ideal for a classic winter soup with a touch of turmeric, which is good for your health. Depending on my mood, I serve it with grated Parmesan or else little croutons or fried bacon cubes."

SERVES 8
Cooking time: 1 hour 10 minutes

1 kg (2 lb.) pumpkin or squash
2 carrots
1 clove of garlic
2 onions
½ tsp. turmeric
Olive oil
Salt, pepper
A few coriander leaves

Peel and deseed the pumpkin, cut into large pieces and steam or boil for 35–45 minutes. Then drain and set aside the flesh.

Peel and slice the carrots widthwise, thinly slice the garlic and the peeled onions and fry them all together in olive oil for 5–10 minutes over a hot flame.

Now add the pumpkin flesh to the pan together with the turmeric, salt and pepper. Cover with cold water and cook for another 15 minutes.

Blend and serve the soup really hot, decorated with a few coriander leaves.

PUMPKIN SOUFFLÉ

"Be warned — all your guests must be sitting at the table for this starter, because a soufflé can't hang around! That's the really difficult thing with this type of dish. Although it doesn't taste much of pumpkin, this autumn soufflé makes a change from the traditional cheese soufflé and its beautiful colour is gorgeous."

SERVES 6
Cooking time: 1 hour

A soufflé dish 21 cm (9 in.)
in diameter

500 g (1 lb.) pumpkin or squash
60 g (2 oz.) butter + a little
for the dish
40 cl (1½ cups) full-fat milk
40 g (1½ oz.) plain flour (T45)
6 egg yolks
7 egg whites
150 g (5 oz.) Parmesan
2 pinches of nutmeg
Salt, pepper

Peel and deseed the pumpkin, cut into large pieces and steam (or bake at 170°C [340°F]) for about 30 minutes. Weigh the flesh — there should be 400 g.

Preheat the oven to 200°C (390°F) (convection position). Butter, then flour the soufflé dish on all surfaces, up to the top. Leave aside at room temperature.

In a saucepan over a gentle flame, heat the milk with the nutmeg, salt and pepper. Beware of adding too much salt: the Parmesan is already very salty. Set aside.

Melt the butter in another saucepan. Add the flour and stir vigorously. Now add the warm milk that has absorbed the nutmeg flavour. Cook until the sauce thickens. Remove from the heat and add the egg yolks one by one, stirring constantly, then the pumpkin flesh and the cheese. Whip the egg whites stiffly and then fold gently into the pumpkin mixture taking care not to lose air.

Check the seasoning and pour into the dish, filling up to three-quarters from the top. Immediately place in the oven and bake for 30 minutes, checking the soufflé without opening the oven door, because otherwise it will fall. Serve immediately.

PUMPKIN GNOCCHI WITH PARMESAN CREAM

"I adore gnocchis — they are so 'moreish'. Especially when they are made with my butternut squash from the vegetable plot! Nicely browned under the Parmesan crust, delicately flavoured with sage, they are perfect for a roast or a veal escalope."

SERVES 6

Cooking time: 1 hour 15 minutes

FOR THE GNOCCHI

A piping bag

550–600 g (17–18 oz.) pumpkin or squash
1 egg yolk
1 egg
230 g (8 oz.) plain flour (T45 or T55)
100 g (3 oz.) grated Parmesan
½ garlic clove
1 pinch of nutmeg
Salt, pepper

FOR THE PARMESAN CREAM

300 g (1 cup + 3 tbsp.) liquid double cream
150 g (5 oz.) grated Parmesan
4–5 sage leaves

Peel and deseed the pumpkin or butternut squash and cut into large pieces. Place in an earthenware dish and bake for at least 40 minutes at 170°C (340°F). The pumpkin flesh, mashed with a fork after leaving the oven, should be as dry as possible. Weigh — you need 450 g (1 lb.).

In a large bowl, mix the pumpkin flesh with the eggs, flour, Parmesan, chopped garlic, nutmeg, salt and pepper. Beat until smooth, then stuff into a disposable piping bag, the end of which should be cut to obtain an opening measuring 2 cm (1 in.).

Boil salted water in a large saucepan. Stand just over it and press the piping bag, then cut off a length of gnocchi with scissors very gently, so that each gnocchi falls into the boiling water. They are cooked as soon as they return to the surface, but count 3–4 minutes of cooking. Remove with a slotted spoon and leave to drain on kitchen paper.

Prepare the Parmesan cream by mixing the cream, Parmesan and sage leaves in a saucepan. Bring to a slow boil over a low flame for about 10 minutes. Finally, remove the sage leaves from the sauce. Arrange the gnocchi in an oven dish and cover with the sage-flavoured Parmesan cream. Allow to brown at 180°C (360°F) for 10 minutes. Serve piping hot.

CHERRY RHUBARB CRUMBLE

"This is a pleasant change from the classic strawberry-rhubarb combo. I use the June harvest of black cherries in this crumble and serve it with vanilla ice cream that melts gently into the tart fruit. Yummy!"

SERVES 8

Cooking time: 40 minutes

500 g (1 lb.) rhubarb
1 kg (2 lb.) black cherries
100 g (3 oz.) caster sugar

FOR THE CRUMBLE

250 g (8 oz.) plain flour
(T45 or T55)
150 g (5 oz.) brown sugar
150 g (5 oz.) softened butter
50 g (1½ oz.) roughly
chopped hazelnuts

Peel the rhubarb with a peeling knife and cut into 1-cm pieces. Rinse the cherries, remove the tails and pit them. Cook the rhubarb with the caster sugar and 2 tbsp. water in a covered saucepan for about 15 minutes over gentle heat.

Preheat oven to 180°C (360°F) and prepare the crumble. In a mixing bowl, place the flour, brown sugar and chopped hazelnuts and then add the butter. Rub in lightly with the fingers until crumbly. Grease an earthenware dish or individual oven dishes and fill with the rhubarb, mixed in with the raw cherries. Then top with the crumble mix and bake for 25 minutes.

Serve warm with crème fraîche or vanilla ice cream.

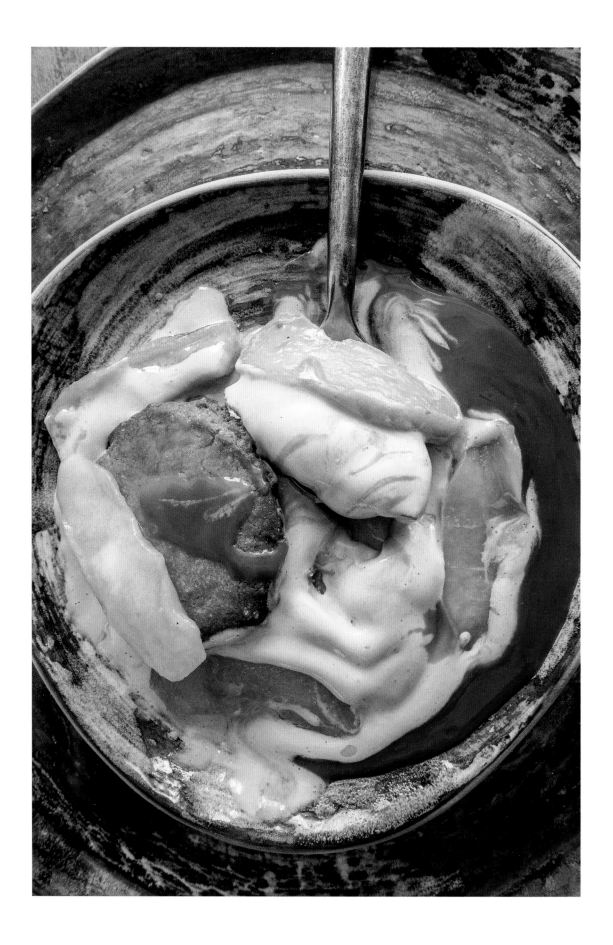

APPLE SHORTBREAD AND CARAMEL ICE CREAM

"Okay, I'll admit this is pretty long to make and it's very difficult to assemble. In fact, I advise you to have several circles for speed, especially if you have lots of guests. It's really an individual dessert that is not particularly easy to eat since you need a knife, fork and spoon! But don't worry, this dessert is actually even nicer and prettier when everything is melting a bit…"

SERVES 8

Preparation: chill the pastry
for 1 hour
Cooking time: 25 minutes

Circles 6 cm (2½ in.) in diameter
and 4 cm (1½ in.) deep

FOR THE SHORTBREAD
(see recipe on page 241)
250 g (8 oz.) plain flour
(T45 or T55)
125 g (4 oz.) softened butter
80 g (2½ oz.) caster sugar
1 pinch of salt
1 egg

FOR THE APPLES
3 Pink Lady or other eating apples
(count ½ apple per person)
150 g (5 oz.) butter
50 g (3½ tbsp.) groundnut oil
6 cl (3½ tbsp.) Cognac
(or Armagnac)

FOR THE TOFFEE SAUCE
200 g (7 oz.) caster sugar
100 g (3½ oz.) butter
50 cl (2 cups) liquid double cream

TO SERVE
Shop-bought caramel ice cream

Prepare the shortbread using Dona's sugar crust pastry recipe on page 241, and refrigerate for one hour. Then roll out to ½ cm (⅛ in.) in thickness and cut out rounds using a circle 6 cm in diameter. Make two biscuits each for six persons. Place them on an oven tray covered with greaseproof paper and bake at 180°C (360°F) for 10 minutes. Remove and cool on a cooling rack.

Peel and cut the apples into fairly thin slices. Heat the butter and oil in a wok or frying pan. Cook the slices, stirring and lifting until cooked but still quite firm. Now add the Cognac or Armagnac, heat for one minute and then flambé. Set aside.

Prepare the toffee sauce. Over a medium heat, melt the sugar with one tbsp. water. When the mixture starts browning, shake the saucepan and quickly add the butter cut into small pieces, then the cooled cream, stirring constantly with a wooden spoon. This sauce can be kept several days.

Place a round shortbread on each plate. Place the circle on it, position a scoop of ice cream in the centre and slide the apples into the space between the ice cream and the circle. Now place the second shortbread on top, press, remove the circle and serve quickly with the warm toffee sauce. You may prefer to serve the sauce in a small separate jug.

POACHED PEACHES
IN VERBENA SYRUP

"Outside my kitchen I planted an enormous lemon verbena bush and I really wanted to recreate its lovely scent in a summer dessert. I found the perfect solution with yellow and white peaches… Add to that a slight touch of elderflower and it becomes a subtle reminder of cool summer evenings!"

SERVES 6
Cooking time: 20 minutes

6 organic white peaches
3 organic yellow peaches
1 large handful of lemon verbena
1 lime
20 cl (¾ cup) elderflower cordial
A little caster sugar (according to taste)
1 handful of mint leaves

Peel the peaches, halve and remove stones, but keep the peelings and stones. Set aside. You may choose to poach the peaches whole if wished.

Place 1 l water in a saucepan with the lemon verbena leaves, the peach peelings and stones and the quartered lime. Boil for 15 minutes, filter, then add the peaches. Boil for 5 minutes, then add the elderflower cordial. Remove from heat and take out the peaches immediately to stop the cooking. Allow to cool. Refrigerate peaches and syrup. If the syrup is not sweet enough for you, add a little caster sugar.

To serve, place one white peach and half a yellow peach in each individual dish (or small pot) and add fresh mint leaves. If wished, the peaches can be accompanied by a scoop of apricot sorbet and a home-made shortbread biscuit.

Aubergines, my favourite vegetable

JAPANESE-STYLE **AUBERGINES**

"I fell in love with this recipe on a trip to Japan with my friend Junko. It is an easy, quick starter and can be served all year. It is delicious with wholemeal rice tea."

SERVES 6

Cooking time: 21 minutes

2 large aubergines
A few sesame seeds

FOR THE MISO SAUCE

3 tbsp. miso
1 tbsp. brown sugar
2 tbsp. saké
2 tbsp. soya sauce
1 cm (½ in.) fresh ginger (optional)
2 tbsp. mirin
Olive oil

Make the sauce ahead of time. In a saucepan, combine the miso, sugar, mirin, sake, soya sauce, grated ginger (optional) and two tbsp. water. Heat to boiling point and keep stirring. When boiling, remove from the heat and set aside to cool at room temperature.

Cut the aubergines lengthwise into slices 1 cm (½ in.) thick. Steam for 15 minutes so that they will not absorb too much oil later.

Heat a little olive oil in a frying pan and fry the slices 3 minutes on each side over a hot flame until they are meltingly soft.

Serve well-browned, pour the tepid miso sauce over the aubergines and sprinkle with sesame seeds.

AUBERGINE **PARMIGIANA**

"For vegans you can replace the Parmesan and mozzarella with tofu mixed with almond milk. But I still prefer this recipe with mozzarella, and the more you reheat it, the better it is…"

SERVES 6

Cooking time: 50 minutes approx.

1 kg (2 lb.) aubergines
Two balls of mozzarella,
125 g (4 oz.) each
50 cl (2 cups) home-made tomato coulis (see recipe on page 248)
100 g (3½ oz.) grated Parmesan
Olive or sunflower oil
1 pinch of dried oregano
Salt, pepper
6 basil leaves for presentation

Rinse aubergines in cold water, cut off ends and peel just one strip of skin from each side. Cut into 1-cm slices. Steam for 25 minutes. In a large frying pan, heat three good tablespoons of olive or sunflower oil. Fry the aubergines quickly over a hot flame for 3–4 minutes on either side. Sprinkle with salt, pepper and oregano. Preheat oven to 170°C (340°F) and build the parmigiana.

Slice the mozzarella. Pour a layer of tomato coulis into a large oven dish, preferably in earthenware, and cover with a layer of aubergine slices. On each slice place a slice of mozzarella. Continue layering tomato coulis, aubergines and mozzarella, topping with grated Parmesan.

Bake for about 20 minutes; the mozzarella should be thoroughly melted and the Parmesan browned.

Serve decorated with a few basil leaves.

LASAGNE AND GRILLED VEGETABLE MILLE-FEUILLE
WITH AUBERGINE CAVIAR

"It's a bit tricky to put together and bite into, but it's really worth it!"

SERVES 6

Cooking time: 10 minutes approx.

6 lasagne sheets
Sunflower or frying oil
500 g (1 lb.) approx. aubergine
caviar (see recipe on page 248)

FOR THE FILLING
1 aubergine
1 courgette
3 tomatoes
1 red pepper
6 asparagus spears
Balsamic vinegar
Sunflower oil
Virgin olive oil
Salt, pepper

Boil water in a saucepan. Cook the lasagne in the boiling water for 2 minutes. Remove and immediately drop into very cold water or water with ice cubes to stop cooking. Dry on kitchen paper and cut each lasagne sheet in two.

Put the sunflower or frying oil into the frying pan and turn up the heat. When the oil is nearly smoking, drop in the lasagne two by two and brown 1 minute on either side. Then drain on kitchen paper to remove the grease. Leave aside.

Now prepare the filling. Cut the unpeeled aubergine and the courgette into rounds about 1 cm thick. Steam or cook in boiling water (about 2 minutes for the courgette and 5 minutes for the aubergine). They should be soft but not overcooked.

Cut the tomatoes into slices 1 cm (½ in.) thick and the pepper into strips.

Heat a frying pan or plancha and brush with sunflower oil. Brown the vegetables 2–3 minutes on either side, season with salt and pepper.

Finally, blanch the asparagus spears very quickly and brown them in the frying pan for 2 minutes, whole if they are small or cut in two lengthwise if they are bigger. Add salt and pepper.

Now build the mille-feuille. Reheat the lasagne in the oven until tepid, the aubergine caviar and the vegetables remaining at room temperature. Lay out one half of a lasagne sheet, spread with aubergine caviar, add two slices of aubergine and build up layers of lasagne, aubergine caviar, tomato, aubergine, courgette and peppers. Drizzle with a little balsamic vinegar and olive oil, then finish with a lasagne sheet spread on one side with aubergine caviar. Decorate the top with a round of aubergine and an asparagus spear. Serve immediately.

FRENCH TOAST WITH AUBERGINES AND FIGS

"When my son Rafou was little, every Saturday or Sunday I made him French toast… So why not try this old-fashioned recipe with aubergines and figs and make a surprising dessert reminiscent of the delicious flavours of childhood?"

MAKES 2 FRENCH TOAST
Cooking time: 35 minutes approx.

FOR THE FIG COMPOTE
4 figs
1 tsp. caster sugar
Juice of half a lime

2 slices of aubergine
2 egg yolks
2 tbsp. caster sugar
1 glass of milk
1 pinch of salt
½ vanilla pod
Butter
Grapeseed or groundnut oil

Peel the figs, place whole in a baking dish and sprinkle with sugar and lime juice. Bake for 30 minutes at 180°C (360°F).

Cut the ends of the aubergine and cut into slices lengthwise ½ cm (⅛ in.) thick. Count one slice per person. Combine the egg yolks, sugar, milk, salt and seeds from the vanilla pod in a bowl, beating well.

Quickly dip the aubergine slices into this mixture and then fry over a high flame for 2–3 minutes on either side in a half-butter, half-oil combination. Drain on kitchen paper.

Place one tablespoon of fig compote on each aubergine slice, roll and close with a toothpick. Serve lukewarm.

AUBERGINE TEMPURA WITH FIG JAM

"I love aubergines but wanted to use them differently. Why not in a dessert? After all, a dessert made of vegetables is rather unusual… My customers hesitate at first, but once they have tried it, they ask for more!"

SERVES 4 (4 TEMPURA)
Cooking time: 2–3 minutes

1 large aubergine
½ glass of cornflour
½ glass of plain flour (T55)
2 tbsp. caster sugar
1 pinch of salt
1 glass of fizzy water
Sunflower oil for frying
Fig jam with citrus fruits
(see recipe on page 124) or
shop-bought fig jam

For four tempura, one aubergine should suffice. Rinse and dry, do not peel, cut off the ends and then cut lengthwise into slices ½ cm (⅛ in.) thick.

Beat the cornflour, plain flour, sugar, salt and fizzy water together into a smooth batter in a bowl.

Heat the sunflower oil to 170°C (340°F) in a deep fryer or large frying pan. Dip the aubergine slices in the batter and fry for 2–3 minutes. Drain on kitchen paper. Present each tempura spread with fig jam.

Country-style recipes

"Today Ibiza is rediscovering its traditions: we are growing more and more local produce and using fewer and fewer chemicals. Among our harvests there are of course our local potatoes, the red and the white ones, with the taste of our countryside where the goats and sheep still graze."

FAN **POTATOES**

"Another way of making our Ibiza potatoes into a chic, tasty dish!"

SERVES 8
Cooking time: 40 minutes

1½ kg (3 lb.) fairly large
potatoes (Roseval,
Belle de Fontenay,
Charlotte, etc.)
Olive oil
1 handful of coarse salt
4–5 bay leaves (optional)
1 head of garlic (optional)

Wash the potatoes and without peeling, cut into two lengthwise. Place the flat side of each potato on a chopping board and cut crosswise and diagonally at ½ cm (⅛ in.) intervals, ensuring that you do not cut right through.

Cover the bottom of an oven dish with the olive oil and salt. Now add all the potatoes flat side down again. If wished, you can add a few bay leaves, slipping them into the slots, and a few unpeeled garlic cloves in the dish.

Bake at 180°C (380°F) for 40 minutes.

ROASTED POTATOES WITH GARLIC

"They are delicious, easy to make and go with meat, fish and salad!"

SERVES 8
Cooking time: 50 minutes

1 kg (2 lb.) potatoes (Roseval,
Belle de Fontenay, Charlotte
or even fingerlings)
1 head of garlic
Olive oil
1 tbsp. coarse salt
A little pepper

Place the whole unpeeled potatoes in a saucepan of cold salted water and cook over medium heat for about twenty minutes. Drain when cooked but still firm, peel and cut into small cubes.

Now put them into an earthenware dish, add the unpeeled garlic cloves, generously cover in olive oil and coarse salt, pepper lightly. Stir and bake at 170°C (340°F) for 20–30 minutes until the potatoes are nicely browned.

THE *TERRASSES* **POTATO PUREE**

"I don't know whether it's the red soil of our island that gives Ibiza potatoes that incomparable flavour, but whatever colour they are, they grow everywhere here and make excellent puree! And of course, at the *Terrasses*, mash is essential with *bacalao*. As I do for tortillas, I cook the potatoes peeled because I find it makes the puree lighter."

SERVES 4
Cooking time: 35–40 minutes

1 kg (2 lb.) potatoes
10 g (2 tsp.) coarse salt
per l (4 cups) water
25 cl (1 cup) full-fat or
semi-skimmed milk
80 g (2½ oz.) butter
8 cl (4 tbsp.) olive oil
A little nutmeg
Salt, pepper

Place the peeled potatoes cut into four large pieces in a saucepan of cold water. Salt the water depending on the quantity. Cover and cook for at least 30 minutes over medium heat. Meanwhile, heat the milk in a saucepan, add the butter and stir until boiling. Remove from the heat. Check the potatoes with a knife point and drain when they are really soft.

Beat the hot potatoes with a whip or push them through the food mill over a saucepan. Add the milk and melted butter, salt and pepper, then the olive oil and a pinch of grated nutmeg. Beat well to a smooth puree. Serve hot.

MY POTATO **GRATIN**

"There's nothing nicer than thinly sliced potatoes cooked in milk and cream and slowly browned in the oven!"

SERVES 8
Cooking time: 1 hour 5 minutes

1.5 kg (3 lb.) firm potatoes
(BF15 or Charlotte)
2 cloves of garlic
1 l (4 cups) full-fat or
half-skimmed milk
10 cl (6 tbsp.) single cream
20 g (½ oz.) butter
1 pinch of nutmeg
Salt, pepper

Peel and thinly slice the potatoes to 3 mm (1/10 in.) thickness. On no account rinse them. Finely chop the garlic and mix in with the potato slices. Place in a saucepan and cover with milk. Season with salt, pepper and a few gratings of nutmeg. Heat over a high heat and cook 4–5 minutes until you see that the starch in the potatoes has thickened the milk. Now add the cream and bring to the boil. Immediately remove and adjust the seasoning.

Butter a large shallow oven dish and spread the potatoes in a layer not exceeding 2 cm (¾ in.) in depth, covering them with the cooking liquid. Bake very gently for at least one hour at 150°C (330°F).

POTATOES WITH PANCETTA AND THYME

"A charmingly rustic dish, or the art of making potatoes, not pigs, in blankets. For even more flavour, you can add a bay leaf slotted in with the branch of thyme."

SERVES 6
Cooking time: 25 minutes

12 small red potatoes
(2 per person)
12 thin slices of pancetta
12 branches of thyme
A few dashes of olive oil
Salt, pepper

Put the whole unpeeled potatoes into a saucepan of cold salted water. Cook over a fairly hot flame. Check with a knife, and when they are cooked but still firm, remove from heat, stop them from cooking with cold water and drain. Cut the two ends of each potato so that it can stand upright. Take a thin slice of pancetta and wrap it around each potato, slipping in a little branch of thyme between the potato and the pancetta.

Place all the wrapped potatoes in an oven dish, drizzle with olive oil, season with salt and pepper and bake at 180°C (380°F) for 3–5 minutes. Serve as an accompaniment to meat or, why not, a fish dish.

POTATOES MASHED WITH OLIVE OIL

"All you need to do is use vegetable milk for this dish to make it completely vegan. This potato mash is good with meat as well as fish, and it has an additional flavour of oats or almond."

SERVES 8
Cooking time: 25 minutes

1 kg (2 lb.) fluffy potatoes
(Bintje or Caesar)
1 pinch of coarse salt
5 cl (3 tbsp.) olive oil
1 pinch of nutmeg
3 cl (2 tbsp.) oat or almond milk
3 drops of lemon juice
3 grinds of the pepper mill
2 garlic cloves (optional)

Peel, wash and cut the potatoes into small pieces, place in cold salted water and boil for about 20 minutes over medium heat. Test softness with a sharp knife. Drain.

Now put them into a pot over a pan of boiling water for 3–4 minutes to keep them warm while you add the oil, nutmeg, vegetable milk, lemon juice and pepper and mash with a fork. This is the moment also to add the crushed garlic if wished. Stir well and serve.

OREGANO **GOAT'S CHEESE FILO**

"We have been serving this almost mythical dish for the past twenty-seven years to our contented customers. I usually serve it as a starter or a light summer lunch with a salad made half of lettuce and half of rocket, seasoned with olive oil and Sherry vinegar, salt and pepper."

SERVES 1
Cooking time: 10 minutes approx.

A slice of goat's cheese 1 cm (½ in.) thick
1 sheet of filo pastry
2–4 oregano leaves (to taste)
Freshly ground black pepper
Sunflower oil

Take a slice 1 cm (½ in.) thick from a large goat's cheese log. (If the cheese log is small, use two slices). In the middle of a sheet of filo pastry, place two or three oregano leaves. Cover with the goat's cheese, pepper and place another oregano leaf on top. Beware — oregano is quite strong, so if you wish, you can put it on just one side of the cheese.

Now fold the filo pastry into a small package: the right side on the cheese, the left side on top of the right, then one side underneath and the last side also underneath and over the third layer. There must be the same thickness above and below the cheese.

Gently heat half a tablespoon of sunflower oil in a frying pan and brown the cheese filo for 1–2 minutes on each side until the cheese is heated through and slightly melting. Finish cooking in the oven at 160°C (320°F or gas mark 3) for 5–8 minutes.

Serve the filo hot on a bed of salad leaves.

SAUTÉED RAVIOLI WITH RICOTTA CHEESE

"We generally serve these ravioli with a spinach leaf salad and a few sundried tomatoes in olive oil. You need four ravioli per person for a starter and six for a main course."

SERVES 8–10
(about 50 ravioli)
Preparation: allow the dough to chill for 1 hour
Cooking time: 5 minutes

A pastry brush

FOR THE RAVIOLI DOUGH
250 g (8 oz.) plain flour (T55)
2 organic eggs
2 pinches of salt

FOR THE FILLING
100 g (3½ oz.) raw chopped ham
(such as Serrano ham)
100 g (3½ oz.) mozzarella
250 g (8 oz.) ricotta
2 organic eggs
50 g (2 oz.) grated Parmesan
1 large bunch of parsley
1 egg yolk
Frying oil
Salt, pepper

First prepare the ravioli dough. Of course, you can buy wonton dough ready-made from a Chinese store, but it is not as nice as home-made. In a large bowl combine the flour, eggs and salt. Knead for 5 minutes in a mixer with a kneading tool or with a whip by hand for at least 10 minutes. The dough must not be sticky. Wrap in cling film and refrigerate for 1 hour.

Meanwhile, prepare the filling. Chop the ham finely by hand, fragment the mozzarella and ricotta, add the eggs, grated Parmesan, chopped parsley, salt and pepper, and mix.

Now make the ravioli envelope. Roll the dough out on a floured board, making it as thin as possible, and cut out squares measuring 8 X 8 cm (3 X 3 in.). On each square, drop one tsp. filling. Dip the pastry brush into the beaten egg yolk and paint the edges of each ravioli before folding and closing them into triangles.

Deep fry these ravioli in hot oil, if possible in two stages: first for 3–4 minutes at 170°C (370°F) and then for one minute at 180°C. Drain on kitchen paper, then serve piping hot with a green salad.

MY COUNTRY-STYLE **TORTILLA**

"My Spanish omelette was inspired from the famous tortilla that you eat in the café-grocery on the Santa Agnès Church square in the heart of the valley of almond orchards. As there are more egg whites than yolks, I figure it is a lot more digestible than traditional tortilla."

SERVES 6

Cooking time: 45 minutes approx.

5 medium potatoes
2 large onions
1 green pepper
1 tomato
9 organic egg yolks
12 organic egg whites
Sunflower oil
Salt, pepper

Peel the potatoes, cut in quarters and cook for about 25 minutes in a saucepan of salted water. Meanwhile, peel the onions, slice and fry in a pan with a little sunflower oil. Add the unpeeled pepper and tomato cut into cubes and allow to cook for 3–4 minutes before removing from heat. Drain the potatoes while still a little firm, cut into smaller pieces and add to the onion, pepper and tomato mix. Set aside.

In a large bowl, combine the 9 yolks and the egg whites. Beat well, season with salt and pepper and add the potato mixture.

Now cook your tortilla. In a large frying pan, heat 2 tbsp. sunflower oil over medium heat and add the egg and potato mixture. After about 5 minutes of cooking, when the omelette seems cooked on one side, place a plate on top of the tortilla and turn the tortilla upside down on the plate. Slide it back into the pan so the other side cooks for at least another 5 minutes.

When your country-style omelette is ready, slide onto a serving dish and eat immediately with a green salad from the garden.

MY GARLIC *FRITA*

"One of my memories of Algeria… Sometimes there is no garlic in frita… Well, whatever you like, but personally, I use it! I also like to fill little pita rounds with it, as a snack or for a picnic."

SERVES 8

Cooking time: 3 hours 40 minutes

2 kg (4 lb.) red peppers
1 kg (2 lb.) home-grown tomatoes
6 garlic cloves
½ tsp. harissa
Salt, pepper
Olive oil

Cook the peppers with their skins in a very hot oven for about 35 minutes, turning halfway through. When they are well cooked and burned, even blackened, place in a plastic bag or sealed container. Leave to cool, then peel and cut into small pieces.

Peel and deseed the tomatoes. Cut into four or eight, depending on the size.

Gently fry the roughly chopped garlic in olive oil in a casserole for 3–4 minutes. Then add the peppers, tomatoes and harissa, seasoning with salt and pepper. Cover and leave to reduce for 2 hours over a very low heat, stirring from time to time. At the end of the two hours, uncover the casserole and allow it to reduce for another hour.

Eat cold as a starter with toast or pita bread.

JUANITO'S *GREIXONERA*

"This milk pudding is a traditional peasant dish in Ibiza and Formentera. Basically, it was a way of using up stale bread and the famous *ensaïmades* that are the Balearic version of croissants. The secret of this *greixonera* was given to me by Juanito, a true *Ibicenco* who is in charge of the desserts at our hotel, and I serve it mostly for breakfast. It's just delicious!"

SERVES 12

Cooking time: 50 minutes

1 l (4 cups) semi-skimmed milk
1 cinnamon stick
1 organic lemon
400 g (14 oz.) caster sugar
6 individual *ensaïmades*
or 6 croissants
8 eggs

Bring the milk, cinnamon, lemon zest and 200 g (7 oz.) sugar to the boil over a gentle heat. At boiling point, remove from the heat and leave to infuse as it cools. When still warm, remove the cinnamon stick and lemon zest and add the *ensaïmades* in small pieces. Beat the eggs and mix into the preparation. Set aside at room temperature.

Preheat the oven to 175°C (350°F or gas mark 4). Melt the remaining 200 g (7 oz.) sugar with 1 tbsp. water in a large, quite deep dish, preferably earthenware. When golden, remove from the heat. Now pour the *ensaïmades* mixture over the nicely browned caramel and bake in a *bain-marie* for about 50 minutes.

Serve this pudding cold.

LA BOMBA
YOGHURT CAKE

"*La Bomba* yoghurt has been sold in Ibiza since 1960. Made with full-fat milk, it has a slightly granular texture that reminds me of Indian yoghurts. A few years ago I used to get it in the old town from an old lady, and I used to fill my jars directly from the churn."

SERVES 8
Cooking time: 35 minutes

1 apple
1 organic orange
2 yoghurt pots filled
with caster sugar
3 yoghurt pots filled
with plain flour (T45 or T55)
2 pinches of salt
½ yoghurt pot filled with
sunflower oil
200 g (7 oz.) *La Bomba* yoghurt
(or 1½ pots filled with full-fat
yoghurt)
60 g (2 oz.) butter
3 eggs
2 tsp. baking powder

Peel the apple and cut it into small cubes. Scrape the zest from the orange.

In a mixing bowl, combine the caster sugar, flour, salt, yoghurt, orange zest, oil, melted butter, whole eggs and finally the baking powder.

Add the small apple cubes and beat well. Pour this batter into an earthenware dish or buttered cake tin and bake for 35 minutes at 180°C (350°F). At the end of the cooking time, leave to cool at room temperature.

In this recipe, you can replace the apples by pears or bananas.

Lunch at my friend Albert's

"Near Cala Salada, my friends
have restored an authentic peasant
finca perfectly, respecting the original
building with its round bread oven
that looks like a brioche dusted
with lime. I love to share my recipes
for the height of summer with them
on days when lunchtime lingers
on beneath the thatched pergola."

SALMOREJO

"This is the true Andalusian gazpacho, practically a meal in itself. Personally, I don't always add the hard-boiled egg if I'm serving it as a starter. However, I don't miss out on the Serrano ham, which must be of excellent quality. I buy it at *Los Andaluces* in Jesús's village."

Quarter the tomatoes and cut the stale bread into small pieces. Place the tomatoes and garlic in the mixer, then add the bread, vinegar, olive oil, salt and pepper. Blend finely and sieve. Refrigerate for 1 hour minimum.

Meanwhile, boil the eggs for 10 minutes in boiling water. Shell them once cold.

To serve the *salmorejo*, crumble a little hard-boiled egg in the centre of the soup and scatter shavings of ham over it. Drizzle with olive oil. Eat very cold.

SERVES 6

Preparation: refrigerate 1 hour before serving

Cooking time: 10 minutes for the eggs

1.5 kg (3 lb.) nicely ripened organic plum tomatoes (Roma)

120 g (4 oz.) stale bread

3 cloves of garlic

5 tbsp. Sherry vinegar (25-year-old reserve)

5 tbsp. virgin olive oil + a drizzle to serve

2 organic eggs

80 g (2½ oz.) shavings of Serrano ham

Salt, pepper

CUMIN LAMB KEBABS,
BLACK RICE OR QUINOA WITH VEGETABLES AND SWEET AND SOUR SAUCE

"This dish may seem rather long to prepare but it manages to combine all the best of two continents. The spicy flavours take us to North Africa and the rice and passion fruit take us to India!"

SERVES 6

Cooking time: about 35 minutes for the rice, 14 minutes for the quinoa and 3 minutes for the kebabs

Kebab skewers

FOR THE RICE

200 g (7 oz.) wild black rice or 200 g (7 oz.) black quinoa
1 onion
1 cinnamon stick
4 cloves
10 cardamom seeds
½ star anise
1 bunch of asparagus tips
1 handful of green beans
1½ yellow pepper
1 red pepper
1 celery stick
1 carrot
1 clove of garlic
1 pinch of cumin
10 chives
1 handful of fresh coriander
Olive oil
Salt, pepper

FOR THE SWEET AND SOUR SAUCE

4 passion fruit
1 tbsp. caster sugar
1 clove of garlic
½ tsp. salt
1 pinch of pepper
1 pinch of hot paprika (optional)
Juice of one lemon (depending on how sharp the passion fruit is)
1 handful of fresh coriander
1 handful of chives

FOR THE KEBABS

600 g (1¼ lb.) deboned leg of lamb
1½ tbsp. cumin
3 tbsp. sunflower oil
Salt, pepper

Wash the wild rice and soak in cold water for 10 minutes. Sweat a peeled, sliced onion in the olive oil over medium heat. Cook the rice in a rice cooker or in a saucepan of salted water for 35 minutes with the cinnamon, cloves, cardamom, star anise and sweated onion. If you opt for quinoa, cook it in twice its volume of water (use a measuring glass), adding the same spices and onion as for the rice. This will cook more quickly (about 14 minutes). The quinoa is cooked as soon as all the water is absorbed.

Meanwhile, peel and halve the asparagus lengthwise and cut all the other vegetables (beans, peppers, celery, carrot) into small pieces or strips. Crush the garlic clove.

In a deep frying pan or a wok, heat a little olive oil over a hot flame and sauté the vegetables for 2–3 minutes with the garlic, salt, pepper and pinch of cumin. Add the cooked rice or quinoa, stir and leave to cook for 2–3 minutes. Just before serving, scatter the top with chopped chives and coriander.

Prepare the sweet and sour sauce.

Cut the passion fruit in two and scoop out the centres into a bowl. Add the caster sugar, the chopped garlic, salt and pepper and, if wished, the paprika. Mix until the juices run. Add the lemon juice if the passion fruit is not tart. Add chopped coriander and chives, and stir.

This sweet and sour sauce should be served in a bowl alongside the rice or quinoa and the lamb kebabs.

Allow for 2 small kebabs per person. Cut the meat into large cubes and season with salt, pepper and cumin. Mix together, adding the oil.

Skewer the meat and fry for 2–3 minutes on each side over a hot flame.

Serve these kebabs with the rice or quinoa with vegetables and the passion fruit sweet and sour sauce.

"Ibiza is an island apart,
a land of freedom where extremes
and different tastes mingle together.
It is ideal for my home cooking
that is bathed in the sunlight of
the Balearics and studded
with flavours picked up here and
there from my travels."

CHERRIES SAUTÉED
WITH ROSEMARY

"This quick, easy recipe was given us by Oriane Gungoa, who worked in the *Terrasses* kitchen for nine years. I have made it even more yummy with pistachio ice cream and my own shortbread."

SERVES 8–10

Cooking time: 5 minutes approx.

1 kg (2 lb.) ripe black cherries
100 g (3½ oz.) butter
1 tbsp. groundnut oil
200 g (7 oz.) powdered sugar
2 stems rosemary
1 *chupito* (small liqueur glass) of rum
Scoops of home-made or shop-bought pistachio ice cream

Wash the cherries, preferably pitting them.

Melt the butter and groundnut oil in a frying pan over gentle heat. Drop in the cherries, sugar and rosemary. Stir or shake the pan vigorously for 4–5 minutes depending on the size of the cherries, and then flambé with the rum.

Serve slightly warm with a scoop of pistachio ice cream and a shortbread biscuit (see recipe on page 244).

SUNNY APRICOT OR PLUM TART

"Despite its ripe fruit brimming with sunshine, this tart is irresistibly crunchy. At the height of the apricot season, my customers at the *Terrasses* often book their tables on condition we're serving our famous tart. What more can I say?"

SERVES 8
Preparation: refrigerate
the pastry for 1 hour
Cooking time: 50 minutes

A tart tin 28–30 cm (12 in.)
in diameter

FOR THE SWEET CRUST PASTRY
(see recipe on page 240)
250 g (8 oz.) plain flour (T45)
80 g (2½ oz.) caster sugar +
1 tbsp. to scatter over the pastry shell
2 pinches of salt
160 g (5 oz.) butter
3 cl (2 tbsp.) water

FOR THE FILLING
1.5 kg (3 lb.) organic apricots or plums
200 g (7 oz.) caster sugar

First prepare the sweet crust pastry following the recipe on page 240. Refrigerate the dough for one hour and just before baking, scatter a tablespoon of sugar over the pastry shell. Bake for 15–20 minutes at 180°C (360°F).

Now prepare the filling. Whichever fruit you use — apricots or plums — the recipe is the same. Rinse the fruit, cut in two and remove stones. Place in a lightly buttered earthenware dish, dust with about 100 g (3½ oz.) caster sugar depending on how tart the fruit is and bake for 15 minutes at 170°C (340°F). Pour off the juice into a saucepan and add 100 g (3½ oz.) sugar. Allow to reduce and thicken over low heat. Set aside.

Arrange the baked apricots or plums in the cooked pastry shell and return to the oven for 10 minutes at 170°C (340°F). At the last minute, pour the reduced juice over the tart. Serve warm — it's even more delicious!

WATERMELON *GRANISADO*

"This is midway between fruit juice and sorbet, and in the height of summer when your throat is parched, it can be drunk with a straw. Fun and cool!"

SERVES 6–8
No cooking

½ watermelon
2 organic lemons
100 g (3½ oz.) caster sugar
4 tbsp. grenadine syrup
(optional)

Deseed the watermelon and crush the flesh in a blender. Add the juice of the two lemons, the powdered sugar and the grenadine syrup if wished. Stir and freeze in an ice cube tray.

To serve, crush in a mixer. Drink this granite with a straw and serve the cool tall glasses with small home-made meringues (see recipe on page 245).

Lunch beneath the fig trees

ROCKET, MANGO, RED CABBAGE AND FIG SALAD

"This is a salad in the pretty colours of late summer. It is crunchy and homespun because of the cabbage, sweet because of the fig, and tart because of the mango and lime. At the *Terrasses*, it is always a success!"

SERVES 4–6

Cooking time: 3 minutes

FOR THE SALAD

100 g (3½ oz.) rocket
¼ red cabbage
1 large mango, not too ripe
6 green asparagus
1 shallot
3 green or black figs
A few coriander leaves

FOR THE DRESSING

2 tbsp. balsamic vinegar
1 lime
4 tbsp. olive oil
Salt, pepper

Wash the rocket and cut the red cabbage into strips and the peeled mango into slices. Peel and cook the green asparagus for 3 minutes in a saucepan of cold water. Then drop into iced water to stop the cooking and drain.

Chop the shallots and cut the figs in two.

In a large salad bowl, combine the rocket, red cabbage, mango slices and chopped shallot. Prepare a salad dressing with the balsamic vinegar, olive oil, lime juice, salt and pepper. When ready to serve, pour this sauce over the rocket, cabbage and mangoes. Mix and add the asparagus and figs. Top with finely chopped coriander leaves.

FIG LEAF-WRAPPED SEA BREAM

"Obviously, you need fig leaves to hand... so off you go for a country walk, because these natural wraps give a fantastic flavour to the bream!"

SERVES 1
Cooking time: 12 minutes

Two wooden or bamboo
toothpicks

1 sea bream, 250 g (8 oz.)
2 slices of fig
1 slice of organic lemon
A few sprigs of fennel
A little olive oil
2 fig leaves
Fleur de sel, milled pepper

FOR THE SAUCE
1 deseeded, cubed tomato
¼ preserved lemon cut very
small (see recipe on page 167)
½ fig cut into cubes
A few basil leaves
Juice of one lemon
1 pinch of Cayenne pepper
Olive oil
Salt, pepper

Preheat the oven to 200°C (390°F). Clean the bream well and decorate with the sliced figs and lemon, adding the fennel branches. Season with salt and pepper, then oil it and wrap it up in the fig leaves, fastening the parcel with two wooden toothpicks. Bake for 12 minutes.

During the cooking, prepare the sauce by combining all the ingredients.

As soon as the bream is cooked, serve with the cold sauce and basmati rice.

LAMB TAJINE WITH FIGS

"In Algeria and Morocco, tajine is very often accompanied by dried figs. Personally I prefer fresh figs when they are in season, of course. The taste is more delicate and they are much prettier."

SERVES 8
Cooking time: 1 hour 15 minutes

A leg of lamb weighing 1½ kg
(3 lb.), cut into pieces, bone-in
3 onions
3 cloves of garlic
1 large bunch of coriander
1 tbsp. cumin
1 tbsp. ground ginger
1 tsp. ground cinnamon
3 cinnamon sticks
½ tbsp. ras-el-hanout
2 tbsp. sesame seeds
2 tbsp. wildflower honey
8–10 green or black figs
Olive oil
Salt, pepper

Sauté the lamb for 8–10 minutes in a little olive oil in a large frying pan or sauteuse over a hot flame until all the pieces are browned on all sides. Set aside.

In the tajine dish, sweat the onions in a little oil, add the finely chopped garlic, half the coriander bunch, salt, pepper, the spices and the honey. Cook over a hot flame for 10 minutes, then add the lamb, two small glasses of water and nearly all the remaining coriander (keep a few leaves to decorate the tajine when serving). Cook over gentle heat for 40 minutes.

Before the lamb is completely cooked, cut the figs in two lengthwise, put them on top of the meat and allow to simmer another 15 minutes. The sauce should be syrupy. Just before serving, scatter the remaining coriander leaves and, if wished, a few more sesame seeds.

FIG **RAVIOLI**

"These ravioli remind me of a posh funfair! Probably because they are crunchy and you bite into them like kids, suddenly coming across the billowy fig hidden inside and getting icing sugar all over your cheeks. They are also reminiscent of donuts at the end of the summer season."

SERVES 8–10

Makes about 20 ravioli
Cooking time: 32 minutes

1 kg (2 lb.) black or green figs
100 g (3½ oz.) caster sugar
The juice of 2 lemons
2 packets of ravioli sheets
(in Chinese groceries)
2 tbsp. liquid wildflower honey
A few oregano leaves
(or failing that, 1–2 tbsp.
dehydrated oregano)
1 egg yolk
Frying oil
A little icing sugar

Peel the figs and cut into small pieces. Combine with the sugar and lemon juice in an oven dish and bake for 20–30 minutes at 180°C (375°F). Remove and allow to cool.

Each ravioli must be made with two ravioli sheets. In the centre of the first, lay a tablespoonful of fig compote, drizzle with liquid honey and top with an oregano leaf (or dehydrated oregano). Brush egg yolk on the surrounding ravioli pastry. Cover with the second sheet and press together on all four sides to seal.

Heat the oil in the deep fryer to 170°C (340°F) and fry each ravioli for 2 minutes. Drain on kitchen paper and dust with icing sugar. Eat immediately.

FIG JAM WITH CITRUS FRUITS

"This is the only fig jam I really like, because the citrus fruits lighten it and add a little acidity. I serve it at breakfast, of course, and I also use it with my aubergine tempura. Then I always hide a few pots in the back of the cupboard for Christmas, so that I can serve it with my home-made goose liver. It is not very sweet so I sterilise the jars and once they are open, I store them in the fridge."

**MAKES ABOUT TEN JARS,
385 ML (15 OZ.) EACH**
Cooking time: 1 hour

2 kg (4 lb.) figs
2 kg (4 lb.) caster sugar
25 cl (1 cup) orange juice
25 cl (1 cup) lemon juice
25 cl (1 cup) grapefruit juice

Carefully peel the figs. Prepare the syrup: combine the sugar and the citrus juices, heat gently and cook for 30 minutes, stirring constantly. Drop in the figs and continue cooking for 20–30 minutes over a low heat.

The jam is cooked when it gells on a plate. Immediately pour it into jars that have been washed and dried beforehand. Sterilise the filled jars so that the jam will keep.

HALF-FIG HALF-RHUBARB TART

"The real plus of this dessert is the combination of sharpness (the rhubarb) with sweetness (the figs). You must try it!"

SERVES 8–10
Preparation: refrigerate the pastry for 1 hour
Cooking time: 45 minutes

A tart tin 30–32 cm (12 in.) in diameter

FOR THE SWEET CRUST PASTRY
(see recipe on page 240)
250 g (8 oz.) plain flour (T45)
160 g (5 oz.) butter
80 g (2½ oz.) caster sugar +
1 tbsp. to scatter over the pastry
2 pinches of salt
3 cl (2 tbsp.) water

FOR THE FILLING
2 kg (4 lb.) green or black figs
1 kg (2 lb.) rhubarb
200 g (7 oz.) caster sugar +
2 tbsp. for the rhubarb syrup

Prepare the sweet crust pastry following the recipe on page 240, line the tart tin and leave to chill without pricking the pastry.

Preheat the oven to 180°C (360°F). Peel the figs and cut into two. Peel and chop the rhubarb into pieces measuring 1 cm (½ in.). In a saucepan, cook the rhubarb quickly (about ten minutes) with the 200 g (7 oz.) sugar and drain in a colander, reserving the rhubarb juice which will be used to make a syrup.

Remove the chilled pastry shell from the fridge, scatter 1 tbsp. sugar over the surface to make it waterproof and bake for 15 minutes at 180°C (360°F).

Meanwhile, heat the reserved rhubarb juice in a saucepan over a medium heat and thicken with 2 tbsp. sugar. Cook until it is a smooth syrup.

When the pastry shell is cooked, remove from the oven, fill with the stewed rhubarb and top with the figs, skin down. Bake for 15 minutes at 160°C (320°F). Leave to cool and when ready to serve, pour the rhubarb syrup over the tart. Eat at room temperature.

FLAMBÉED FIG
AND ROSEMARY KEBABS

"I owe this recipe to my cook Roshan. He wasn't really a pastry cook but he knew how to whip up a dessert from three figs and some rum… These kebabs are such a good idea — the art of improvising an original, spectacular and delicious dessert in a trice!"

Cut the rosemary branches to the desired length. Slide two or three whole figs onto each one. In a frying pan, melt a large lump of butter with a little oil over a low heat. Put in the fig kebabs, scatter a little sugar and a few more sprigs of rosemary over them and sauté for 2 minutes on every side.

Transfer the kebabs to the oven for about 8 minutes at 190°C (375°F). Meanwhile, heat a small liqueur glass of rum, pour it over the kebabs and flambé immediately on serving.

SERVES 4
(4 kebabs)
Cooking time: 10 minutes

A few branches of
rosemary
8 nicely firm green or black
figs (2 per kebab)
1 or 2 lumps of butter
Groundnut oil
A little caster sugar
1 liqueur glass of rum

Tuesday is Couscous Day

"This couscous has become a ritual. Every Tuesday for the past 22 years, we have served it to our hotel guests, of course, but also to all the couscous fans on the island. I learned the recipe and how to roll the couscous grains with Aïcha in Algeria, back in 1975. Later, at the *Terrasses*, it was Sarah who added her own flair and, over the years, we have adjusted and improved it so that it is as digestible as possible. I think the most important thing is to cook the various meats separately, and the vegetables are what make the bouillon. As for the couscous grains, the adventure starts on Mondays when we get out our huge pans so that we can roll the couscous as the Algerian or Moroccan women do."

THE *TERRASSES* **COUSCOUS**

SERVES 10

One couscous pan with a capacity of approx. 11 l (22 pints)

COOKING TIMES:

2 hours 45 minutes for
the reduced onions
About 35 minutes for the pumpkin
6 hours 20 minutes for the bouillon
About 1 hour 20 minutes for
the vegetables
About 13 minutes for the meatballs
45 minutes for the chicken
6 minutes for the kebabs
10 minutes for the merguez
20 minutes for the couscous grains
Time for reheating

FOR THE REDUCED ONIONS

3 kg (6 lb.) yellow onions
4 tbsp. groundnut oil
100 g (3½ oz.) raisins
300 g (10 oz.) caster sugar
2 cinnamon sticks

FOR THE BOUILLON

2 kg (4 lb.) yellow onions
1 kg (2 lb.) tomatoes
4 celery sticks
2 fingers of fresh ginger root
1 tbsp. mace
1 bay leaf
1 bunch of coriander
1 bunch of parsley
2 tbsp. home-made spice mix
(see below)
1 bird's eye chilli
2 cloves of garlic
Groundnut oil
Salt
Pepper (optional)

Step-by-step preparation

1 Prepare the reduced onions the day before

To save time, make this the day before. Peel and thinly slice the onions, then sweat in 4 tbsp. oil over a hot flame for 10–15 minutes, stirring constantly. Continue cooking at lower heat and allow the onions to reduce slowly in the covered pan for two hours. Before the end, add the raisins. When the onions are ready, add the caster sugar and cinnamon sticks. Continue slow cooking for another 30 minutes.

2 Prepare the bouillon

Peel and slice the onions and fry in oil over a medium heat for 10 minutes. Add all the other ingredients: the unpeeled tomatoes cut in quarters, sliced celery sticks, peeled and sliced ginger root, mace, bay leaf, coriander, parsley, home-made spice mix, chillies, garlic and salt. Stir-fry over a hot flame for 15–20 minutes, then place in the bottom half of the couscous pan, adding 3 litres cold water. Check seasoning, pepper lightly if necessary. Cover and cook for 6 hours over a low flame, adding water when necessary. Drain the bouillon into another large pan using a small ladle if required.

3 Steam the pumpkin

Cut the unpeeled pumpkin in half, remove seeds and cut into ten large pieces. Steam for 30 minutes. Once cooked, dust with sugar, salt and cinnamon and place in the steam cooker again for 5 minutes. Leave aside at room temperature.

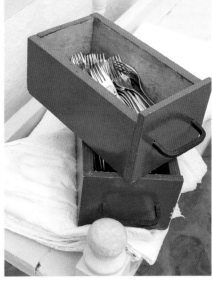

"On the famous Couscous Day,
the entire hotel swings into action,
with clattering pots in the kitchen and
rushing about on the terrace; every week
there is the same upheaval! Even during
siesta time, our hive of busy little bees
buzzes around the slumbering guests,
preparing the tables for the evening
feast in every little corner of the garden,
producing a swarm of white tables."

FOR THE PUMPKIN

1 kg (2 lb.) pumpkin
2 tbsp. caster sugar
½ tsp. salt
1 tbsp. ground cinnamon

FOR THE VEGETABLES

1 kg (2 lb.) savoy cabbage
1 kg (2 lb.) carrots
1 kg (2 lb.) turnips or christophines
1 kg (2 lb.) courgettes
1 tsp. home-made spice mix
(see below)
20 *pimientos de padrón*

FOR THE MEATBALLS

300 g (10 oz.) crustless, slightly stale
brown bread
600 g (1¼ lb.) ground veal or beef
2 large onions
½ handful of parsley
1 large handful of mint leaves
1 clove of garlic
2 eggs
½ tsp. salt
½ tsp. pepper
¼ tsp. ground nutmeg
½ tsp. ground cumin
A little flour
Sunflower oil

FOR THE MEAT

Wooden skewers
800 g (1 lb. 12 oz.) leg of lamb
(fat removed) for the kebabs
10 chicken drumsticks
Sunflower oil
2 lemons
20 merguez
Salt, pepper, ground cumin,
ground nutmeg

4 Cook the vegetables

Remove the outer leaves from the cabbage, cut into large pieces, parboil in salted boiling water for 30 minutes, then drain. Peel the other vegetables: the carrots, courgettes and turnips (or christophines), ensuring that the courgette skin is peeled in stripes. Drop all these vegetables into the re-heated bouillon, starting with the carrots and turnips (or christophines), and finally the courgettes. Remove from the bouillon as soon as they are well cooked and lastly, drop in the drained cabbage pieces, to which you have added a teaspoon of the spice mix. Cook for 10 minutes until tender, then set aside with the other vegetables.

The *pimientos de padrón* should be fried at the last minute.

5 Prepare the meatballs

First soak the crustless brown bread (preferably a bit stale) in cold water for 30 minutes. Combine the mince with the finely diced onions, parsley and mint, together with the drained bread and all the other ingredients: the garlic, whole eggs, salt, pepper, nutmeg and cumin. Shape into balls of around 80 g (2½ oz.), roll in flour and fry in a little sunflower oil in the frying pan over a high flame for 10 minutes, turning regularly so that they brown all over. Be careful not to overcook them because at the last minute you will be deep frying them. Meanwhile, refrigerate until needed.

6 Prepare the lamb kebabs

Cut the leg of lamb into cubes, removing the fat, and marinate in the fridge with 1 tsp. salt, ½ tsp. pepper and 1 tsp. cumin for one hour. Then thread the marinated cubes onto wooden skewers. Count one skewer per person. Set aside.

7 Prepare the chicken

Place the drumsticks in an oven dish, pour 3 tbsp. sunflower oil over them and sprinkle with 1 tsp. salt, a scant tsp. pepper, a rounded tsp. cumin, ½ tsp. nutmeg and the juice of the two halved lemons (remember to keep the lemon rinds, which will be used in the cooking). Marinate the drumsticks for 1 hour in the fridge, then add the lemon rinds and bake at 180°C for 30 minutes. Remove, turn over the meat and return to the oven for a further 15 minutes.

FOR THE HOME-MADE SPICE MIX

(All these spices to be blended in the food mixer or pounded in the mortar)
2 tbsp. mild Cayenne pepper
1 tbsp. turmeric
1 tbsp. ground ginger
¼ tbsp. ground cinnamon
½ tsp. ground nutmeg
1 tbsp. ground coriander
½ tbsp. ground cumin
½ tsp. cloves (crushed or ground)

FOR THE COUSCOUS GRAINS
1 kg (2 lb.) high-quality, medium-grain hard wheat couscous
2 tbsp. groundnut oil
40–60 cl (2–2½ cups) water
Salt

TO SERVE
A little harissa
1 bunch of coriander

8 Prepare the merguez

Prick the merguez and pre-cook in an oiled pan over a high flame for 10 minutes, turning regularly. Drain, discard excess fat and leave aside.

9 Prepare the couscous grains

Of course, the couscous grains are much nicer when rolled by hand. At the *Terrasses*, we roll them three times and we start off the day before. However, until you learn this delicate skill, use the best-quality medium grain possible and the most traditional method possible. Pour the couscous grains into a bowl, add two tbsp. oil and 40–60 cl (2–2½ cups) cold water. Allow the water to soak in. Then boil up around 1.5 litres (3 pints) of water in the bottom half of the couscous pan (which you used for the bouillon). Mix the couscous grains, rolling them with the fingertips to separate them, and place in the upper half of the couscous pan. Cook for ten minutes. Then roll again with the fingertips, season and allow to cook for another ten minutes. Once everything is cooked, discard the water from the bottom half of the pan.

10 Final assembly

Before serving, return the chicken to the oven for 15 minutes and the merguez for ten minutes to heat through.

Cut the vegetables into large pieces, pour the bouillon into the lower half of the couscous pan and heat it with all the vegetables including the cabbage. Meanwhile, deep-fry the meatballs for 3 minutes and sear the kebabs for 3 minutes on each side in a frying pan. In another frying pan or deep-fryer sauté the *pimientos de padrón* for about 2 minutes, stirring constantly. Heat up the pumpkin in the microwave for 2 minutes (or 5–10 minutes in the oven at 170°C [340°F]).

When everything is hot, drain the vegetables and in a large shallow dish present the vegetables and *pimientos* on one side and the chicken, kebabs, meatballs and merguez on the other. One attractive presentation is to skewer the turnips with the kebabs.

Pour the piping hot bouillon into a large bowl and decorate with 3 or 4 stems of roughly cut coriander. Present the hot couscous grains in another large bowl.

In separate, smaller bowls, serve the reduced onions and the pumpkin. Finally, don't forget to serve the harissa in a small dish. Bring all the dishes to the table at the same time, so that the guests can help themselves as they wish.

In the almond orchards

ALMOND AND DATE *TAJINE*

"This is a classic, but to give it a bit more flavour, I add *Sirop de Liège*, which is simply a jam made from fruit such as dates."

SERVES 6

Cooking time: 1 hour 10 minutes

A leg of lamb weighing
1.5 kg (3 lb.), bone-in and cut
into pieces

1 large handful of peeled
almonds

3 onions

3 garlic cloves

1 tbsp. cumin

1 tbsp. ground cinnamon

½ tbsp. ras-el-hanout

1 bunch of coriander

2 glasses of white wine

2 handfuls of dates

2 tbsp. olive oil

Salt, pepper

Ask your butcher to cut a leg of lamb into 12 pieces with the bone in. Roast the dry almonds quickly on an oven tray for 5–6 minutes at 170°C (340°F). Set aside.

In a large shallow pan, heat two tbsp. olive oil and brown the lamb pieces. When browned all over, set aside, but discard the bones and cooking oil.

Peel and cut the onions into small pieces, fry in the same pan and add the crushed garlic, spices, half the chopped coriander, white wine, salt and pepper. Allow to simmer for 15 minutes over a low flame and then add the lamb pieces and cover with a little water. Continue cooking over a low flame for 40 minutes, covering the pan and stirring from time to time.

10 minutes before the end of the cooking time, scatter the pitted dates over the dish and, to serve, sprinkle with the almonds and the rest of the chopped coriander.

Serve with couscous or boiled potatoes.

MARIA'S *TARTA DE SANTIAGO*

"Maria, Juanito's mum, is a true *Ibicenca* grandma. She gave him the secrets of this tart, which is typical of the Santiago de Compostela region, where the almond trees bloom in the byways, a bit like here in the Valley of Santa Agnès de Corona. The great thing about this recipe is that it doesn't contain butter, only almonds."

SERVES 10–12

Cooking time: 40 minutes
A cake tin measuring
23 X 35 cm (10 X 14 in.)

450 g (1 lb.) caster sugar
500 g (17 oz.) powdered almonds
6 g (1 heaped tsp.) ground cinnamon
1 pinch of salt
1 organic lemon
10 eggs
1 tbsp. icing sugar
(for decoration)
1 knob of butter to grease the cake tin

Preheat oven to 170°C (340°F). In a mixing bowl, combine the sugar with the powdered almonds, cinnamon, salt and finely grated lemon zest. Gently fold in the eggs one by one.

Grease the tin before filling and bake for approx. 40 minutes at 170°C (340°F).

When the cake has cooled, dust with icing sugar, decorating if wished by making a stencilled pattern out of greaseproof paper.

ALMOND **BLANCMANGE**

"Originally this was a Caribbean blancmange, but I turned it into an Ibizan blancmange by substituting almonds for the grated coconut. I serve it with a strawberry or raspberry coulis, easily prepared by blitzing red fruit, a little sugar and the juice of one lemon."

SERVES 8

Cooking time: 5 minutes approx.

250 g (8 oz.) fresh peeled almonds

15 cl (9 tbsp.) water

15 cl (9 tbsp.) full-fat or semi-skimmed milk

220 g (8 oz.) caster sugar

10 g gelatine (5 sheets) or 1½ tsp. agar-agar (with 2 tbsp. water)

40 cl (1½ cups) liquid double cream

Strawberry or raspberry coulis to taste

Almonds, strawberries or raspberries for decoration (optional)

Soak the gelatine sheets in very cold water for 10 minutes or dilute the agar-agar in 2 tbsp. cold water.

Grind the almonds in a mixer, gradually adding 15 cl (9 tbsp.) water. Leave the mixer running and add the milk to form a smooth paste. Place the mixture in a saucepan with the sugar and heat gently, stirring constantly, to dissolve the sugar. Just before it comes to the boil, add the drained, softened gelatine — or the agar-agar, which is a more natural gelling agent. In the latter case, boil for 2 minutes, stirring well. In both cases, leave aside to cool for 15 minutes at room temperature.

Whip the cream until it thickens. Incorporate it into the cooled preparation. Pour into small glasses, individual dishes or a large mould and refrigerate for several hours.

If you have chosen a large mould, dip it into hot water and unmould by turning out onto the service plate. Decorate to taste with an almond, strawberries or raspberries and serve with a red fruit coulis. This blancmange keeps 2–3 days if well covered in the refrigerator and can thus be prepared in advance.

Choccy desserts – Clara and Alice's favourites

A GOURMAND'S CHOCOLATE MOUSSE

"There's nothing nicer than a chocolate moustache! Like me and my clients, my granddaughters Clara and Alice are chocaholics and they are always there to lick my big bowls when I make this mousse. The secret of the recipe is temperature. The chocolate must melt gently and the egg yolks must not be added until it has cooled to 30°C (82°F)."

SERVES 8

Preparation: at least 6 hours ahead of time
Cooking time: 10–12 minutes

400 g (14 oz.) dark chocolate (maximum 55% cocoa solids)
80 g (2½ oz.) butter
7 egg yolks + 9 egg whites (preferably organic eggs)
1 tbsp. Cognac or Armagnac (optional)

Break the chocolate into small pieces and melt in a double saucepan or microwave with the butter. Monitor the temperature and stir if needed, because the chocolate must melt but not cook. When it is melted, remove and allow to cool at room temperature, stirring occasionally. When the chocolate is tepid (30°C [82°F]), add the egg yolks and the Cognac or Armagnac. Mix and set aside.

In a mixing bowl, whip the egg whites until they form peaks. Then gently fold them into the chocolate mixture, lifting and turning with a wooden spoon or a spatula. Pour into a serving bowl or individual bowls. Refrigerate for at least 6 hours.

GIANT CHOCOLATE MACAROONS

"These are nothing like normal macaroons, which are merely a mouthful… Mine are much bigger and fatter: you'll get at least five mouthfuls… Divine!"

SERVES 8

Preparation: leave the mixture to cool for 3 hours and the ganache for 2 hours

Cooking time: 30 minutes

FOR THE MACAROONS

200 g (7 oz.) dark chocolate (53–55% cocoa solids)

200 g (7 oz.) ground almonds

200 g (7 oz.) icing sugar

4 egg whites

FOR THE GANACHE

200 g (1 cup) liquid double cream

200 g (1 cup) chocolate (57–65% cocoa solids)

Preheat the oven to 170°C (340°F). Melt the chocolate in a double saucepan or in the microwave turned down low. Remove from the heat when melted and add the powdered almonds and three-quarters of the icing sugar. Mix.

Whip the egg whites (no need for them to form peaks) and fold in the rest of the icing sugar. Fold this mixture into the chocolate mixture. Finally, and this is very important, refrigerate for three hours. Meanwhile, prepare the ganache. In a saucepan, heat the liquid cream. Before it boils, add the chocolate broken into small pieces, cover and remove from the heat until the chocolate melts. Return to a gentle heat if necessary. Then beat the mixture and refrigerate for about 2 hours.

Once the macaroon mixture has rested, remove from the fridge, grease an oven tray covered with greaseproof paper and, using an ice cream scoop, form 16 drops of dough. Bake for 14 minutes at 180°C (350°F). Remove from the oven and cool on a cooling rack.

To serve, assemble the macaroons. Take one macaroon half and place the curved side down. Spread with a good spoonful of ganache and cover with another macaroon half. Serve or keep refrigerated.

THE TERRASSES *BROWNIES*

"Young or old, everyone fights for these — at the *finca*, my brownies are not just reserved for kids! I like to serve them with a ganache, the one I use to fill my chocolate macaroons. They are pretty good with a custard, too!"

MAKES ABOUT 24 BROWNIES
Cooking time: 30 minutes approx.

500 g (1 lb.) chocolate
(53–55% cocoa solids)
400 g (14 oz.) butter
300 g (10½ oz.) icing sugar
200 g (7 oz.) plain flour (T45)
7 organic eggs
1 handful of shelled green
pistachio nuts
1 handful of mixed shelled walnuts
and hazelnuts
2 tbsp. bitter cocoa powder

Melt the chocolate with the butter in a double saucepan (or in the microwave on low). Then add the sugar, flour, beaten eggs and nuts. (Cut the walnuts and hazelnuts into two but leave the pistachios whole).

Grease a large oven tray and pour in the mixture. Bake for 30 minutes at 175°C (350°F). Leave to cool, dust with cocoa powder and cut into pieces depending on how greedy you are!

MY CHOCOLATE **MADELEINES**

"This favourite is the *Terrasses*'s version of Proust's madeleine. My customers adore them and they are among their best memories of their holidays. Every year they come back for more, especially when they are served slightly warm with a scoop of vanilla ice cream."

MAKES 20–24 MADELEINES
Preparation: leave the dough
to rest for at least 1 hour
Cooking time: 25 minutes

A madeleine tray

200 g (7 oz.) unsalted butter
80 g (2½ oz.) plain flour (T45)
100 g (3½ oz.) icing sugar
80 g (2½ oz.) finely ground
peeled almonds (or shop-
bought ground almonds)
40 g (1½ oz.) chopped
hazelnuts
180 g (6 oz.) dark chocolate
(57% cocoa solids)
6 whites of large eggs
1 tbsp. mild acacia honey

In a large saucepan, melt the butter over medium heat for 5 minutes, keeping your eye on it, until it begins to brown slightly. Dip the bottom of the saucepan in cold water to stop the cooking.

Sieve the flour and sugar into a bowl and add the almonds and hazelnuts. Melt the chocolate in a double saucepan or the micro-wave, monitoring the temperature closely. It must melt, not cook.

Whip the egg whites lightly, as for making tuiles. Fold the flour-sug-ar-almond-hazelnut mixture into the egg whites, whip and then add the butter and honey and finally the melted chocolate.

Prepare the madeleine tray by greasing with butter, then flouring. Fill each mould with a large tbsp. of mixture and refrigerate for at least 1 hour (this is important — otherwise the inside of the made-leine will overcook). Then bake at 180°C (350°F) for 14 minutes. The madeleines should not blacken. Unmould with a sharp knock and allow to cool on a cooling rack.

MY CHOCOLATE **TART**

"This is a must for the true chocaholic! However, beware — it is difficult to get out of the mould, so I advise serving it straight from there."

SERVES 8–10
Preparation: allow dough
to chill 1 hour
Cooking time: 1 hour 15 minutes

An oblong tin or a round tart
tin 28 cm (10 in.) in diameter

FOR DONA'S SUGAR CRUST PASTRY
(see recipe on page 241)
250 g (8 oz.) plain flour (T45 or T55)
125 g (4 oz.) softened butter
80 g (2½ oz.) caster sugar
1 pinch of salt
1 egg

FOR THE FILLING
40 cl (1½ cups) liquid double cream
1 tbsp. full-fat milk
400 g (14 oz.) dark chocolate
(60% cocoa solids)
2 large eggs
Bitter cocoa powder (optional)

Prepare Dona's sugar crust pastry recipe (see page 241) an hour ahead of time if possible. If you like, line the tart tin and refrigerate so that it is ready to bake.

Preheat the oven to 180°C (360°F). Bake the pastry shell blind for 15 minutes, then take it out of the oven to cool without removing from the tin. Lower the oven temperature to 100°C (212°F).

Combine the cream and the milk in a saucepan. Bring to the boil, remove from the heat and add the chocolate broken into small pieces. Stir until the chocolate has melted completely, then leave to cool. When the mixture is tepid, add the lightly beaten eggs one by one and whip until smooth.

Pour the chocolate mixture into the pre-cooked pastry shell and bake for about 50 minutes at 100°C (212°F). Monitor the filling, which should be set but still slightly wobbly in the centre.

Serve the tart at room temperature, lightly dusted with cocoa if wished.

MY CHOCOLATE *DULCE DE LECHE*

"Originally from South America, *dulce de leche* is a sort of very sweet milk jam that reminds me of my childhood. I have given it a personal touch with a scoop of chocolate sorbet and a little amaretto liqueur that gives it a bitter almond flavour."

SERVES 8

Cooking time: 7 minutes

250 g (8 oz.) granulated sugar +
2 cl (0.4 cup) cold water to make caramel
2 drops of lemon juice
850 g (4 cups) liquid double cream
8 scoops of chocolate sorbet
A few pinches of *fleur de sel*
24 drops of amaretto liqueur
Some strands of saffron

Make the caramel. Pour the granulated (or caster) sugar, cold water and lemon juice into a saucepan. Bring to the boil without stirring over a medium flame. When the caramel begins to brown, gently shake the saucepan without splashing the edges. When the caramel is nicely brown, after about 7 minutes, remove from the heat. Stop it from cooking by pouring in the cream very carefully. Mix well. Allow to cool and then put in the refrigerator for at least 2 hours. To serve, pour the caramel cream into bowls or soup plates. In the centre of each, put a scoop of home-made or shop-bought chocolate sorbet and decorate with a pinch of *fleur de sel*, three drops of amaretto liqueur and a few strands of saffron. Serve quickly before it melts!

CHOCOLATE **SORBET**

"This is the sorbet I serve with my *dulce de leche*, but it is so irresistible that chocaholics adore eating it on its own, along with their expresso and a shortbread biscuit."

SERVES 8

Cooking time: 5 minutes

An ice cream maker or turbine

120 g (4 oz.) caster sugar
200 g (7 oz.) dark chocolate
(53–60% cocoa solids)
80 g (2½ oz.) bitter cocoa powder

In a saucepan, combine the caster sugar with ½ l (2 cups) mineral water. Heat over a moderate flame, stirring until the sugar has melted. Now add the chocolate broken into pieces and mix. Remove from the heat as soon as the chocolate has melted. Add the cocoa powder, stir and allow to cool. Pour into an ice cream maker or turbine to freeze.

Citrus season

LAMB TAJINE WITH PRESERVED LEMONS

"This is a flashback to my years in Algeria… I like the combination of lamb with preserved lemon because it sharpens and illuminates the dish with a shaft of Mediterranean sunshine! For an even more Middle Eastern note I serve it with home-made pita bread."

SERVES 6

Cooking time: 1 hour 10 minutes approx.

A leg of lamb weighing 1.5 kg (3 lb.), bone-in and cut into pieces
3 onions
3 cloves of garlic
1 bunch of fresh coriander
2 tbsp. ground ginger
1 tbsp. ground cinnamon
1 cinnamon stick
1 tsp. ras-el-hanout
4 preserved lemons
2 glasses of white wine
Olive oil
Salt and ground pepper

Buy a leg of lamb at the butcher's and ask him to cut it into 12 large pieces, bone-in. Sear the meat in olive oil in a casserole or tajine over a high flame. When it is browned, remove the meat and bones and discard the oil.

In the same casserole, fry the sliced onions in two tbsp. olive oil. Add the peeled garlic, half the bunch of coriander, one tsp. salt, the spices and several turns of the pepper mill. Cook over a medium flame for 15 minutes.

Now add the browned meat together with two preserved lemons cut into quarters, the white wine and a little water. Simmer over low heat for about 45 minutes until the lamb is meltingly tender. To serve, discard the lemons from the cooking pot and replace them with the other two fresh preserved lemons cut in four. Also remove the coriander and the cinnamon stick. Arrange the meat in a dish and scatter the remaining fresh coriander leaves on top.

Serve very hot with couscous or boiled potatoes.

FATIMA'S MUM'S *PRESERVED LEMONS*

"Fatima, who has worked for many years at the *Terrasses*, is in charge of preserved lemons. Her Moroccan mother gave her the trick. Twice a year, in winter and then spring, Fatima preserves pounds and pounds of lemons that will be used later, mostly in tajines."

FOR A 3 L JAR (6 PINTS) THAT CAN CONTAIN AROUND A DOZEN LARGE LEMONS

Preparation: 1–2 months before using

12 organic lemons
24 tsp. coarse salt
1 bay leaf
1 branch of thyme
3 or 4 small chillies
Some olive oil

Clean the jar you are going to use in very hot water and dry. Boil a large saucepan of water for five minutes, then leave to cool. This will later fill the jar. Wash the lemons and half-cut into quarters, ensuring the cuts allow the lemons to stay whole but open like flowers.

Take the first lemon, open it up and pour two teaspoons of coarse salt into the centre, in the heart of the four quarters. Close up tightly and place in the jar. Repeat for all the lemons, pressing down as tightly as possible in the jar. In between, slip in the bay leaf, the thyme and three or four chillies.

Gently pour in the boiled water but do not fill to the top. Leave about two centimetres and top up with olive oil. Close the lid of the jar tightly and turn the jar upside down, leaving for 24 hours. The next day, turn the jar back up and leave the lemons to soak for one, or better two, months before using.

With this method, the lemons can keep outside the fridge for a year if the jar is tightly closed. Once it has been opened, place the lemons in the fridge.

"I love citrus fruits in tarts or jams — they restore you to health. There is nothing like them for giving you a draught of sunlight! On Ibiza, we have wonderful lemons almost all year round, but I avoid orange juice at the height of summer because we tend to look after the avocado trees then and ignore our orange trees."

DONA'S *ORANGE CAKE*

"Dona was a friend of my mother Henriette. She was good at baking and this light, moist cake was one of her recipes."

SERVES 6

Cooking time: 25 minutes

A baking tin 24 cm (10 in.)
in diameter

80 g (2½ oz.) softened butter
+ a little for the tin
220 g (7½ oz.) caster sugar
(120 g [4 oz.] + 100 g [3½ oz.]
for the syrup)
3 eggs
120 g (4 oz.) plain flour
(T45 or T55)
Rounded tsp. baking powder
3 organic oranges

FOR THE CANDIED ORANGE PEEL

2 organic oranges
2 tbsp. caster sugar

Preheat oven to 180°C (375°F or gas mark 4). Place the softened butter and 120 g (4 oz.) sugar in the food mixer and mix until white and fluffy. Add eggs, flour and baking powder. Mix until smooth, then add the zest of two oranges and the juice of one orange. Mix again.

Turn the mixture into the baking tin lined with lightly buttered greaseproof paper. Bake for 20 minutes at 170°C (340°F). Take out the cake, cover with aluminium foil and bake for a further five minutes approx. at the same temperature. Test the centre with a knife, which should come out clean.

While the cake is cooking, juice the remaining two oranges, sieve and pour into a saucepan with 100 g (3½ oz.) sugar. Heat slowly, stirring regularly.

Once the cake is cooked, remove from the oven, turn out onto a serving plate and soak with the sweetened orange juice. Leave to cool. Serve with candied orange peel decoration if desired.

To make the candied orange peel, peel the oranges and cut the peel into narrow strips. Place in a saucepan, cover with water and quickly bring to the boil. Remove the strips immediately. Then place in another saucepan with two tablespoons of sugar and simmer gently for ten minutes. Drain, then use the strips to decorate the orange cake.

THE TERRASSES *LEMON TART*

"The classic lemon tart is often topped with meringue. Personally, I prefer it without any additions, just plain, with organic products. The subtle flavours and sunny zing of the lemons stand out so much more."

SERVES 8–10

Preparation: chill the dough
for one hour
Cooking time: 1 hour 6 minutes

A tart tin 28 cm (12 in.)
in diameter

FOR DONA'S SUGAR CRUST PASTRY

(see recipe on page 241)
250 g (8 oz.) plain flour
(T45 or T55)
125 g (4 oz.) softened butter
80 g (2½ oz.) caster sugar
1 pinch of salt
1 egg

FOR THE FILLING

1 organic orange
3 organic lemons
3 eggs
1 egg yolk
150 g (5 oz.) caster sugar
15 cl (9 tbsp) double cream

Prepare the sugar crust pastry following the recipe on page 241. Line the greased and lightly floured tin with the pastry, pressing gently with fingers. Refrigerate this shell for at least one hour. Then bake the shell blind for about 16 minutes at 180°C (360°F). Remove from the oven and allow to cool in the tin.

Now prepare the lemon filling. First squeeze the orange and lemon juice. Beat the whole eggs, egg yolk and sugar together. Add the juices and then the cream. Whip well. When the mixture is frothy, pour half into the pre-cooked pastry shell. Place the tart on the oven shelf, then finish filling up to the edges of the shell with a spoon to avoid spillage when placing in the oven.

Bake at 100°C for 50 minutes. Check the firmness of the lemon flan by slightly shaking the tin. It should not wobble. At the end of the cooking time, leave to cool at room temperature before eating.

ORANGE AND LEMON *MARMALADE*

"This is the jam we serve at the *Terrasses*. Never a breakfast goes by without my orange and lemon marmalade! I always make it in February — it's my special ritual. I cook it up for the whole season and there are boxes and boxes of jars on the top of the scullery cupboards."

MAKES TWENTY-FIVE JARS,
50 CL (1 LB.) EACH

Preparation: two sessions, with
24 hours refrigeration
Cooking time: approx.
2 hours 45 minutes + 35 minutes
sterilisation

16 large organic lemons

25 organic oranges

5 kg (11 lb.) granulated sugar
(1.5 kg [3 lb. 5 oz.] for the lemons
and 3.5 kg [7 lb. 11 oz.] for
the oranges)

Water to cover the fruit +
60 cl (2½ cups) water for
the lemon syrup

First prepare the lemons.

Cut the ends off the lemons and peel them, taking a little bit of pith. Then slice thinly, put in a saucepan and cover with water. Refrigerate for 24 hours.

On the following day, bring the lemons to the boil, stirring regularly. Then stop the heat and leave to cool a little. Drain, change the water and cook again for about 20 minutes at medium heat, stirring regularly, until the lemon pith is soft. Discard the water.

Heat 60 cl (2½ cups) water and 1.5 kg (3 lb.) granulated sugar, add the lemons and cook a further 30 minutes over gentle heat, stirring all the while.

Now prepare the oranges.

Cut off and discard the ends and partly peel the fruit. Slice thinly, keeping the remaining pith, place in a saucepan and cover with water. Then add 3.5 kg granulated sugar. Refrigerate for 24 hours. The next day, place the orange mixture in a large jam pan and cook for one hour over a very low heat, stirring regularly.

Then add the lemons to the orange mix and cook the mixture for 30 to 45 minutes over a gentle heat, still stirring, until the jam looks shiny and the fruit is cooked through.

When the jam is ready, ladle it immediately into the boiled jars (to do this, boil water, pour it into the jars, close them and turn upside down, leaving for 5 minutes, then empty out the water). Seal the pots and sterilise them for at least 35 minutes at 100°C. This jam has low sugar content, so the jars must be sterilised for storing. Once the jar is open, remember to keep it in the fridge.

FATIMA'S MUM'S *PRESERVED LEMONS*

"Fatima, who has worked for many years at the *Terrasses*, is in charge of preserved lemons. Her Moroccan mother gave her the trick. Twice a year, in winter and then spring, Fatima preserves pounds and pounds of lemons that will be used later, mostly in tajines."

FOR A 3 L JAR (6 PINTS) THAT CAN CONTAIN AROUND A DOZEN LARGE LEMONS

Preparation: 1–2 months before using

12 organic lemons
24 tsp. coarse salt
1 bay leaf
1 branch of thyme
3 or 4 small chillies
Some olive oil

Clean the jar you are going to use in very hot water and dry. Boil a large saucepan of water for five minutes, then leave to cool. This will later fill the jar. Wash the lemons and half-cut into quarters, ensuring the cuts allow the lemons to stay whole but open like flowers.

Take the first lemon, open it up and pour two teaspoons of coarse salt into the centre, in the heart of the four quarters. Close up tightly and place in the jar. Repeat for all the lemons, pressing down as tightly as possible in the jar. In between, slip in the bay leaf, the thyme and three or four chillies.

Gently pour in the boiled water but do not fill to the top. Leave about two centimetres and top up with olive oil. Close the lid of the jar tightly and turn the jar upside down, leaving for 24 hours. The next day, turn the jar back up and leave the lemons to soak for one, or better two, months before using.

With this method, the lemons can keep outside the fridge for a year if the jar is tightly closed. Once it has been opened, place the lemons in the fridge.

TASTES OF **THE SEA**

My island's octopus and calamari

OCTOPUS À LA GALLEGA

"Originally this was a speciality from Galicia in northwestern Spain. Today, octopus à la Gallega is one of the commonest tapas throughout Spain, simply seasoned with paprika and a little coarse salt that crunches when you bite into it."

SERVES 4
Preparation: at least 1 day ahead of time
Cooking time: 45 minutes

A cork (placed in the cooking water, it makes the squid tender)
Wooden toothpicks or skewers

1 kg (2 lb.) octopus
(freeze in advance if possible)
4 garlic cloves
2 bay leaves
1 celery stick
1 carrot
1 large onion
3 cloves
3 potatoes
Olive oil
Fleur de sel
Salt, pepper

Remember to buy the octopus a few days ahead and freeze it to make it tender. For this recipe, use only the large tentacles. Put them in a big pot with lots of water and add the unpeeled garlic, bay leaves, celery stick cut in two, peeled and sliced carrot, peeled and clove-studded onion, salt, pepper and finally the cork, which will tenderize the squid. Cook for 20 minutes over a medium flame, then add the peeled whole potatoes. Continue cooking for another 25 minutes. Drain everything.

Cut the still-warm potatoes into rounds. Cut the meatiest part of the tentacles into slices and place on the potatoes. Drizzle with a little olive oil, sprinkle with paprika and *fleur de sel*, and provide toothpicks in the centre.

Serve warm as tapas or a starter.

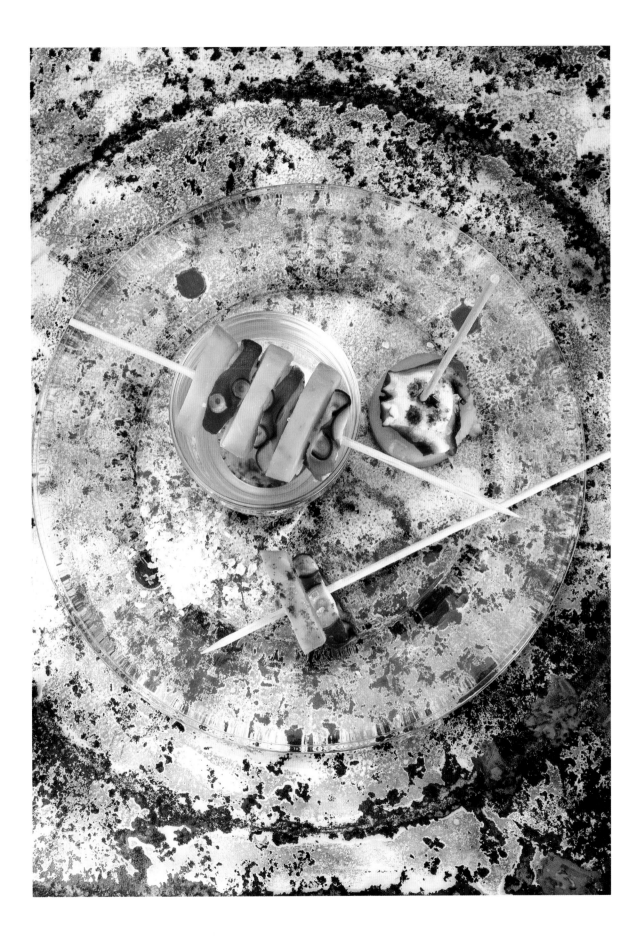

CALAMARI WITH COURGETTES AND LIME

"I sometimes serve these calamari with a salad made of avocados, spring onion stems and green asparagus seasoned with lime and olive oil… It's even nicer then!"

SERVES 6
Cooking time: 9–10 minutes

2 calamari
2 kaffir leaves (combava,
Thai lemon leaves)
1 courgette
1 red onion
1 clove of garlic
1 small chilli
1 lime
A few coriander leaves
A few basil leaves
Salt, ground pepper
Groundnut oil

Slice the thoroughly cleaned calamari into rings. Remove the backbone of the kaffir leaves. Slice the unpeeled courgette and the onion into thin rings.

Heat a little groundnut oil in a pan and fry the calamari over a hot flame for 5 minutes. Salt lightly.

In another frying pan, sauté the onion in 2 tbsp. oil over a hot flame for 1–2 minutes, then add the garlic and crushed chilli, together with the courgette and the kaffir leaves. Continue cooking for another minute.

Just before serving, add the calamari, mix and cook everything for one minute over the hot flame. Present the dish with a few slices of lime and top with coriander, basil, tiny slices of chilli and a turn of the pepper mill.

MAURITIUS-STYLE OCTOPUS SALAD

"This is a lovely cool salad brought back from his native island by my cook Roshan Gungoa. Believe me, octopus salad with our famous Ibiza potatoes is perfect for our summer lunches between land and sea."

SERVES 6
Cooking time: 1 hour

4 small potatoes
1 kg (2 lb.) octopus
1 onion
3 cloves
2 pinches of ground cinnamon
4 tomatoes
1 small tumbler of lime juice
1 tbsp. mild paprika
A few coriander leaves
3 sprigs of parsley
Olive oil
Salt, pepper

Peel the potatoes and steam or boil in salted water. Clean the octopus and put it in a large pot of cold water along with the clove-studded onion, the cinnamon, salt and pepper. Boil for 45 minutes without covering, drain the octopus, allow to cool and cut into tiny pieces.

Cut the tailed and deseeded tomatoes and the potatoes into small cubes. Combine with the octopus and season with the olive oil, lime juice, salt, pepper and paprika. Add a few coriander and parsley leaves and serve well-chilled.

CUTTLEFISH-CALAMARI KEBABS
WITH *JABUGO* AND BLACK RICE

"With the cuttlefish ink, the rice alone already has the aroma of the sea… So imagine the whirl of flavours when you add a cuttlefish-calamari kebab with the famous Spanish *jabugo* ham!"

SERVES 6

Cooking time: 15 minutes approx.

Wooden kebab skewers

2 fairly thick slices of *jabugo*
500 g (1 lb.) cuttlefish
500 g (1 lb.) calamari

FOR THE RICE

2 cloves of garlic
5 shallots
300 g (10 oz.) pudding rice
Strongly diluted shop-bought
fish stock (1½ volume to 1 volume
rice, i.e., 450 cl [10 pints])
Two packets of 10 g (⅓ oz.)
cuttlefish ink each (from
the fishmonger or frozen)
Olive oil
Salt, pepper
Parsley (optional)

Leave the skewers to soak in water. Chop the previously grilled *jabugo* ham, the cuttlefish and the calamari into large pieces. Thread onto the skewers alternately.

In a frying pan, heat 1 tbsp. olive oil over medium heat and sauté the garlic, sliced shallots and rice. Add the hot fish stock gradually and as soon as it boils, add the ink.

The rice is cooked when the liquid has been completely absorbed. It should still be a little crunchy.

Before the end of cooking, heat a grill or a fairly large pan. Rub with olive oil and fry the kebabs very quickly on either side. Season with salt and pepper and serve with the black rice. Top with parsley if wished.

CASSEROLED **OCTOPUS**

"I adore taking this surprise casserole with me when I go to picnic in my friends' boathouse in winter. It's all ready: all you have to do is heat it up for 10 minutes on a makeshift gas ring, then you break the crust and, oh! what a feast, what a gift from the sea!"

SERVES 6

Cooking time: 2 hours 30 minutes

At least 2 kg (4 lb.) octopus
6 potatoes
20 cl (¾ cup) white wine
or cider vinegar
20 grains of pepper
3 bay leaves
4 unpeeled garlic cloves
1 tbsp. coarse salt
1 small chilli
4 cloves stuck into an onion
200 g (7 oz.) plain flour

Use a casserole with an air vent to let the steam escape. Wash the octopus, remove the eyes and put the whole thing into the casserole with all the ingredients: the peeled potatoes, vinegar, pepper, bay leaf, garlic, coarse salt, chilli, onion and cloves.

Mix the flour into a thick paste with a glass of water and roll out a long sausage. Stick it along the edge of the casserole before putting on the lid so it is sealed.

Bake for 2–2½ hours depending on the size of the octopus in a very low oven (150°C [300°F]).

To serve, break the crust, remove the lid and it's ready to eat!

CALAMARI STUFFED WITH *SOBRASADA*

"*Sobrasada* is our Balearic variety of chorizo! This pork sausage may be mild or spicy, depending on how much paprika you put in. Sometimes Ibizans eat it as it is, raw on bread, but I can't do it! However, as a stuffing for calamari or as accompaniment to scallops, *sobrasada* is just perfect."

SERVES 6

Cooking time: 40 minutes approx.

Wooden toothpicks

12 calamari max. 15 cm (3½ in.) long
A little olive oil

FOR THE STUFFING

60 g (2 oz.) whole almonds
1 bunch of parsley
6 shallots
6 garlic cloves
1 red pepper or 2 *noras*
(small mild peppers)
150 g (5 oz.) *sobrasada*
1 egg
Sunflower oil
Salt, pepper

FOR THE SAUCE

12 small tomatoes
1 onion
3 garlic cloves
1 sprig of thyme
1 bay leaf
1 bird's eye chilli
Olive oil
Salt

Carefully clean the calamari. Separate the bodies, heads and tentacles. The body will be stuffed. Throw away the head and keep the tentacles for the stuffing, chopping into small pieces. Drain the calamari bodies and tentacles thoroughly.

Make the stuffing. Fry the almonds in a little sunflower oil over a gentle flame and finely chop them with the parsley, shallots, garlic, pepper, *sobrasada* and calamari bits. Season with salt and pepper and sauté everything for 3 minutes over a medium flame. Remove, add the egg to bind and stir this stuffing well.

Prepare the sauce. Peel and crush the tomatoes. Chop the onion and garlic and, in a large frying pan, sauté in a little olive oil over a hot flame. Add the tomatoes, thyme, laurel and bird's eye chilli. Salt lightly. Leave to simmer for 20 minutes.

Meanwhile, stuff the calamari bodies with the *sobrasada* mix and secure each one with a wooden toothpick. Brown the calamari quickly in a little olive oil in a frying pan over a hot flame.

When everything is ready, combine the calamari with the sauce in the large pan and continue cooking with a lid for 15 minutes over low heat. Serve with rice.

My table in the fishing shack overlooking the sea

"My other house is a small,
ramshackle fishing shack that
overlooks the Mediterranean,
perched on the rocks above
Cala Salada on the west side of
the island. It's my refuge, my boat
leaving for faraway places.
There, shaded by the roof decking,
the whole family gathers to chill
out and share the taste of the sea
together."

IBIZA *PESCADO* SOUP

"This is the traditional recipe of Ibizan and Balearic fishermen. It is a soup prepared with very simple fish, but they are supremely fresh. The plus? We add almonds and cinnamon!"

Bake the almonds in an oven dish or tray for 10 minutes at 160°C (320°F). Set aside.

Rinse the fish and crabs in running water. Peel the carrots and celery and cut into large pieces. Quarter the unpeeled tomatoes. Finely slice the garlic and take a long ribbon 1 cm (½ in.) wide of peel from the orange.

Fry the onions with the fish and crabs in a little oil in a casserole over a hot flame for 10 minutes. Then add the carrots, celery, tomatoes, garlic, thyme, bay leaves, orange peel, pastis, salt and pepper. Cover completely with water and cover and simmer gently for one hour. Then blend and press through a sieve. Towards the end, pour water into the sieve to extract a maximum of fish. Check seasoning.

Grind the almonds, mix with the ground cinnamon and add to the soup. Stir and serve with small garlic croutons fried in olive oil and a little aïoli.

SERVES 6

Cooking time: 1 hour 20 minutes

100 g (3½ oz.) peeled almonds
1 kg (2 lb.) rockfish and
small fish for the soup
2 spider crabs
2 carrots
1 celery stick
500 g (1 lb.) tomatoes
2 cloves of garlic
1 organic orange
2 onions
1 sprig of thyme
2 bay leaves
1 tbsp. pastis
½ tsp. ground cinnamon
A few garlic croutons
1 bowl of aïoli (optional)
Olive oil
Salt, pepper

ROSHAN'S **ACCRAS**

"I think of these as tapas, but from tropical islands — Reunion Island, the Caribbean and even the Balearics! The recipe was given to me by one of my former cooks, Roshan, from Mauritius. These savoury, deliciously crunchy appetisers are perfect for buffets in summer."

SERVES 6
Preparation: chill the mixture for 2–3 hours
Cooking time: 10 minutes approx.

250 g (8 oz.) desalted cod
125 g (4 oz.) plain flour (T45)
2½ tsp. baking powder
10 cl (6 tbsp.) full-fat milk
1 bunch of spring onion stems
1 handful of parsley
¼ tsp. chilli paste
Deep frying oil
Salt, pepper

FOR THE SAUCE
200 g (7 oz.) tomatoes
30 g (1 oz.) fresh ginger
¼ tsp. chilli paste
2 cloves of garlic
½ bunch of coriander
½ small tumbler of water
2 g (¹/₃ tsp.) salt
2 g pepper

In a saucepan, cover the desalted cod in water, bring to the boil and then drain. Break into small pieces and add the flour, baking powder, milk, finely chopped spring onion stems, parsley leaves, salt, pepper and chilli paste. Mix well and cover with a damp cloth. Then chill for 2–3 hours.

Just before serving, heat the oil in a deep fryer. Using two tablespoons, shape small balls of the mixture and slide into the hot oil. One accra contains about half a tablespoon of the mixture. When the accras float up to the surface, continue cooking for two minutes. As soon as they are well browned, remove and drain on kitchen paper.

You can serve these small puffs piping hot with a sauce you made beforehand by whizzing the unpeeled tomatoes, ginger, chilli paste, peeled garlic cloves, coriander, water, salt and pepper through the blender.

LIGHT SOUP OF UDON NOODLES
WITH SHELLFISH

"A Japanese friend made this recipe for me one night. If you add rocket, this nouvelle-cuisine Japanese starter becomes Mediterranean. It should be prepared a little ahead of time and must be served chilled."

SERVES 6

Preparation: at least 4 hours ahead of time
Cooking time: 20 minutes approx.

1 kg (2 lb.) shellfish (clams, carpet shells or scallops)
1 l (2 pints) ready-made dashi stock (in packets) or to make it: 1 tbsp. *katsuobushi* shavings (dried bonito) and 1 sheet kombu seaweed
1 packet of dried udon noodles (275–300 g, 9–10 oz.)
2 handfuls of rocket
2 tbsp. mirin
1 spring onion stem
½ tsp. sesame seeds
¼ lime per person

At least 4 hours ahead of time, put the shellfish into a basin of salted cold water to let the sand sink to the bottom. Then rinse in running water.

Prepare the dashi stock. If you are making it yourself, put 1 litre (2 pints) water into a saucepan and add the *katsuobushi* and the seaweed. Cook gently for about 10 minutes, making sure the liquid never boils and then sieve.

Return the stock to the heat and drop in the shellfish to open them. Remove the shellfish and set them aside at room temperature. The stock must be kept and refrigerated.

Meanwhile, cook the udon noodles in salted water following the instructions on the packet. Drain and add ice cubes. Allow to cool at room temperature, allowing the ice cubes to melt.

When ready to serve, put the noodles mixed with the shellfish and rocket into individual soup plates or bowls. Add the mirin to the stock and pour it over the mixture. Scatter with chopped spring onion stems and a few sesame seeds.

Serve chilled with a quarter lime in each bowl.

TAHITI FISH

"This is a souvenir of a fantastic trip to Tahiti… In fact, I didn't intend to put the recipe in the book, but last winter I went to a sunny island with friends and family and they all clamoured for this dolphinfish practically every two days, because it is so wonderful to eat with your fingers, wrapped in a salad leaf, while you loll back in the sand. And anyway, we have a lot of dolphinfish in Ibiza that are good with this recipe."

SERVES 6

Preparation: at least 5 hours
ahead of time
No cooking

800 g (1½ lb.) fillets of sea bream,
delicious dolphinfish,
or any other firm whitefish
500 g (1 lb.) approx. coarse salt
5 tomatoes
2 spring onions
⅓ tin of 400 ml (scant 1 cup)
coconut milk
1–2 bird's eye chilli
3 limes
A little coriander
A dozen lettuce leaves
Chilli paste to serve
(optional — see recipe
on page 249)
Olive oil

Cut the fish fillets into small cubes, mix thoroughly with the coarse salt and refrigerate for at least 5 hours. Before using, rinse thoroughly in cold water. Cut the tomatoes and onions into small cubes. Combine the coconut milk with 2 tbsp. olive oil, the chillies cut into small pieces and the juice of two limes. Add the tomatoes, onions and then the fish. In theory, you will not need to add salt.

Serve on chilled plates. On each plate, lay two lettuce leaves, drizzle with olive oil and place the fish-onion-tomato mixture in the centre. Top with a little chopped coriander and a few slices from the remaining lime.

Also serve a small bowl of Roshan's chilli paste (see recipe on page 249) for those who like spicier food.

CRAB SALAD

"Was it crab legs and shells that inspired this recipe? Maybe, because I wanted a salad that crunched and here everything is crunchy — the cucumber, the celery and the kohlrabi."

SERVES 6
No cooking

250 g (8 oz.) crab meat
A 200 g (7 oz.) tin of crab legs
½ Chinese cabbage
2 celery sticks
1 cucumber
1½ avocados
1 kohlrabi
5–6 lettuce leaves
3 spring onions
A few coriander leaves
Mixed seeds (sesame, sunflower, squash, linseed, etc.)
Spring onion stems (optional)

FOR THE SAUCE
1 tsp. sesame oil
2 tbsp. olive oil
1 tbsp. balsamic vinegar
Juice of 2–3 limes
1 tbsp. soya sauce
Salt, pepper

You can prepare the sauce ahead of time, combining all the ingredients. Drain the crab meat. Then clean all the vegetables. Cut the Chinese cabbage into strips, peel and finely slice the celery, cut the cucumber in half, deseed and cut into fine strips. Peel and finely slice the avocados and cut the kohlrabi into tiny sticks. Finally, cut the lettuce and onions into small pieces.

When all your vegetables are ready, mix them and add the drained crab meat and a few coriander leaves.

Divide the salad into small bowls, drizzle with a little sauce and decorate with the crab legs, a few mixed seeds and, if wished, the chopped spring onion stems.

SHELLFISH
WITH BASIL AND THAI LEMON

"I ate something very similar in Thailand, but with prawns. I reinterpreted the dish using our shellfish that are abundant at Ibiza's market. It is one of my favourite starters when I serve oriental dinners."

SERVES 6

Preparation: at least 4 hours
ahead of time
Cooking time: 5 minutes

1 l (2 pints) shellfish
(clams, carpet shells, etc.)
1 tbsp. white vinegar
(or 1 tbsp. coarse salt)
2 cloves of garlic
½ red chilli
1 handful of basil
1 sprig of thyme
3 branches of lemongrass
2 small tomatoes
2 fingers of fresh ginger
4 kaffir leaves (Thaï lemon)
4 tbsp. nuoc-mâm
1 handful of coriander
1 tbsp. groundnut (or sunflower
or coconut) oil

At least four hours ahead of time, put the shellfish into a large bowl of cold water with a tablespoon of white vinegar or coarse salt. The sand will decant to the bottom of the bowl. Then rinse the shellfish thoroughly in running water.

Chop the garlic and red chilli, roughly chop the basil, strip the thyme, cut the lemongrass into two lengthwise, cut the peeled tomatoes into small cubes and thinly slice the ginger.

In a wok, heat a tablespoon of oil and when it is nearly smoking, throw in the shellfish. Add the tomatoes and the red chilli, garlic, basil, thyme, kaffir leaves, ginger, lemongrass and nuoc-mâm. Stir constantly over a hot flame for 3–4 minutes. When the shellfish are open, divide up into six bowls, top with the fresh basil and coriander, and serve immediately.

RED MULLET WITH POTATOES

"A mixed land-sea dish that looks good and sandwiches the delicate flavour of a small wild red mullet between two layers of sweet-tasting Ibiza potatoes."

SERVES 4
Cooking time: 35 minutes approx.

4 large potatoes (1 per person)
12 red mullet fillets
4 rosemary sprigs with long stems
A small lump of butter
1 tbsp. pastis
Olive oil
Salt, pepper

Cook the potatoes in their skins in a saucepan of cold salted water on normal heat.

Prepare, or ask your fishmonger to prepare, the red mullet fillets, making sure all the small bones are removed with tweezers.

When the potatoes are cooked, peel and cut into thick slices lengthways.

In an oven dish oiled with olive oil, build your "red-mullet-potato sandwiches" as follows:

Take a slice of potato, then two red mullet fillets, season with salt and pepper, then add a slice of potato and finish with one red mullet fillet. Season and fix with a rosemary branch stuck through all the thicknesses of the sandwich to keep it in place and flavour it too.

Bake in a hot oven for 12 minutes.

Meanwhile, melt the lump of butter with the pastis in a frying pan. Pour this mixture over the sandwiches to serve.

SARDINES IN LIME

"This is a good way to prepare sardines with no hassle and no smells: it's just serendipity!"

SERVES 8
Preparation: the day before
No cooking

1 kg (2 lb.) sardines
8 juicy limes
Coarse salt
Olive oil
Pepper
Chives or parsley (optional)

The day before, remove the sardine heads, cut in two in the thickness and remove the backbones (or ask the fishmonger to prepare them). Take a bowl or terrine and cover the bottom with coarse salt. Cover with a layer of sardines, skin side down. Cover with salt. Add on another layer and continue in layers until the last, which should be salt. Refrigerate for 24 hours.

The next day, rinse the sardines two or three times in cold water until there is not a speck of salt left. Squeeze six limes and cover the sardines with the juice. Drain it off after one hour.

When ready to serve, arrange the sardines in a dish and sprinkle with the juice of the two remaining limes and a drizzle of olive oil. Add a little salt if needed, and pepper, chives or parsley according to taste. You can also add a few slices of lime to decorate.

"On Ibiza, all the salt from the sea seems to have crystallised on the surface of the pink ponds in its nature reserve Ses Salines. Our Ibizan salt harvest is an age-old industry. At the Torres family's small workshop, they dry the tiny white grains in the sun, as they have since time immemorial between June and September, when the piles of *fleur de sel* rise like mountains in white overcoats and then all we have to do is fill the salt grinder."

ORIENTAL-STYLE SEA BREAM

"I gave this simple, delicious recipe to my daughter-in-law who is not yet a very experienced cook. Now she shows off to all her friends! The best part is that, despite the sesame oil and soya sauce, the flavour of the fish comes out very strongly."

SERVES 1

Steaming time: 14 minutes approx.

One 250–300 g (8–10 oz.)
sea bream per person
4 thin slices of ginger
1 lemongrass stick
1 stem of spring onion
A few chopped coriander leaves
2 tbsp. soya sauce
1 dessertspoonful of sesame oil
Pepper
Chilli paste to serve (optional —
see recipe on page 249)

Clean the bream or ask the fishmonger to clean it. Thinly slice the ginger. Clean the lemongrass by removing damaged leaves and cutting out the hard part. Chop the spring onion stem into diagonal slices as done in Asia and set aside.

Make two cuts into the bream flesh on either side. Slip the ginger slices into these and the lemongrass into the inside of the fish. Place the fish in a wooden or metal steamer or in a steam oven. Keep a careful eye on the cooking, for it is essential. In a steam oven, you should count 14 minutes.

Present the bream in a serving dish, top with all the chopped spring onion, a little chopped coriander and a generous amount of the soya sauce and sesame oil mixture. Season with ground pepper and serve immediately, accompanied by white Thai rice.

You can also serve this with a small bowl of chilli paste (see recipe on page 249) for those who like spicy food.

SPANISH-STYLE MUSSELS

"These are eaten all along the Spanish coast in the *chiringuitos* on the seashore or at the market *puestos de tapas*. Spanish mussels are particularly large, but our small cultivated mussels also work for this recipe."

SERVES 4
Cooking time: 15 minutes approx.

1.2 kg (3 lb.) large mussels
2 onions
3 cloves of garlic
3 tomatoes
1 carrot
1 sprig of rosemary
A few bay leaves
10 cl (6 tbsp.) dry white wine
A few parsley leaves
Sunflower oil

Clean the mussels. Peel and slice the onions and garlic. Cut the tomatoes and carrots into small pieces.

In a casserole, heat sunflower oil over a hot flame. Sauté the onions and garlic, then add the carrots, tomatoes, rosemary, bay leaves and white wine. Cover and cook for 10 minutes.

Add the mussels, cover and continue cooking, stirring from time to time, until the mussels open. When they are ready, sprinkle with parsley and serve immediately.

SCRAMBLED EGGS WITH **SEA URCHINS**

"You have to wait until the end of August and the waning summer to be able to eat what I love most in all the world — sea urchins! Before that, it is forbidden to fish for them in Ibiza... So when the shore gradually returns to peace, we often go swimming near the flat rocks at Cala Salada and collect these wonderful sea creatures, and we eat them with scrambled eggs when we get back to the cabin."

SERVES 6
Cooking time: 3–4 minutes

18 sea urchins
9 fresh organic eggs
2 tbsp. liquid whipping cream
Salt, pepper
A little chopped parsley

Open the sea urchins with scissors and rinse in seawater or salted water, making sure you remove the black parts. Break all the eggs into a bowl and quickly beat in the cream.

Prepare a double boiler. Place the beaten eggs and cream seasoned with salt and pepper in the non-stick thick-bottomed upper pan and begin stirring with a wooden spoon. Quickly add the sea urchin tongues and continue stirring until the mixture resembles thick cream. It cooks quickly, in 3 or 4 minutes.

Serve quickly, after topping with a little chopped parsley and a few extra sea urchin tongues just to make it prettier!

MONKFISH STIR-FRY
WITH VEGETABLES AND COURGETTE FLOWERS

"What better way to flavour and enhance a fish than with a basketful of vegetables from the garden?"

SERVES 6

Preparation: marinate at
least 3 hours
Cooking time: 20–25 minutes

1 kg (2 lb.) monkfish (or grouper,
swordfish or white tuna)
3 tomatoes
4 carrots
1 courgette
1 red pepper
1 green pepper
2 large potatoes
4 courgette flowers
2 unpeeled garlic cloves
1 flat tbsp. ground ginger
3 tbsp. sunflower oil
3 tbsp. olive oil
3 pinches of salt
3 turns of ground pepper
A few coriander leaves

FOR THE MARINADE

2 chopped garlic cloves
4 tbsp. chopped coriander leaves
4 tbsp. olive oil
1 tsp. ground cumin
2 tsp. ground paprika
1 pinch of saffron
½ tsp. Cayenne pepper
½ tsp. salt

Combine all the ingredients of the marinade. Cut the fish into large pieces and marinate them for 3 hours in the fridge. Keep two tbsp. of marinade for the cooking.

Meanwhile, peel the tomatoes and cut into large quarters, then sauté in the olive oil. Peel the carrots, courgettes and peppers and cut into sticks. Peel the potatoes and cut in half. Blanch the carrots and potatoes for a few minutes in salted boiling water, then drop into freezing water. Drain.

Heat the sunflower oil in a wok and throw in all the vegetables and the unpeeled garlic. Leave to cook for 2 minutes. Remove and set aside. Now put a little olive oil in the wok, add the fish, the two tbsp. of marinade and the tbsp. of ginger, and stir-fry for 3–4 minutes on each side. Once it is cooked, remove the monkfish from the wok and put back the reserved vegetables, season with salt and pepper and leave to cook 3–4 minutes. Right at the end of cooking, add the courgette flowers after removing the pistils. Then add back the fish pieces. To serve, top with fresh coriander leaves.

MAURITIUS CURRY AT THE BEACH CABIN

"I love Mauritius. I find it a haven of peace with its magnificent colours and the sea, the friendliness and the scents. Everyone cooks this dish over there, and when you go into a house it is redolent of spices, because there is always a huge black pot simmering away on the wood fire. It's wonderful! So, to keep up the impression of being in Mauritius, I cook this curry in my beach cabin on Ibiza."

SERVES 6

Cooking time: 1 hour 15 minutes
+ 30 minutes for the stock

FOR THE SPICE MIX

50 g (1½ oz.) coriander seeds
15 g (3 tsp.) cumin seeds
10 g (2 tsp.) mustard seeds
5 g (1 tsp.) ground cinnamon
60 g (2 oz.) turmeric
20 g (4 tsp.) white pepper seeds
10 g (2 tsp.) cardamom seeds
5 g (1 tsp.) cloves

FOR THE FISH STOCK

The remains of the cleaned fish
1 carrot
1 celery stick
1 large onion
1 handful of parsley
1 sprig of thyme
2 bay leaves
Salt, pepper

FOR THE TOMATO *CHATINI*

300 g (10 oz.) tomatoes
1 onion
1 clove of garlic
½ tsp. chilli paste
(see recipe on page 249)
A little olive oil
2 pinches of salt

FOR THE FISH

1.2 kg (3 lb.) white, fairly firm fish
such as grouper or monkfish,
cleaned, headless and tailless,
cut into steaks
2 onions
1 tbsp. chopped garlic
2 tbsp. chopped fresh ginger
20 g (4 tsp.) spice mix (see above)
4 tomatoes
1.5–2 l (3–4 pints) fish stock
(shop-bought or home-made)
2 bay leaves (or karipouley,
if you are on Mauritius)
Olive oil
Salt
A few fresh coriander leaves

Combine all the spices in a dry frying pan and shake for about 3 minutes over a gentle flame, then whirl in a mixer and put aside in a closed jar.

Now prepare the fish stock. You can buy this or make your own. In the latter case, keep the head and remains of the fish once cleaned and sliced into steaks or ask your fishmonger to do this. Put all the remains in a large pot with the sliced carrot, celery stick, onion, parsley and thyme, plus the bay leaves. Fill up with 1.5–2 litres water (3–4 pints), season with salt and pepper, cover and cook for 30 minutes over a medium heat. Set aside; it will be used to cook the curry.

The *chatini* is quite spicy and will serve to sharpen up the curry. Peel and cut all the ingredients — tomatoes, onion and garlic — into very small pieces. Add a little chilli paste and a dash of olive oil. Salt lightly. Set aside in a small bowl.

Now prepare the fish curry. In a large casserole, sauté the fish steaks quickly in a little hot olive oil, 2–3 minutes on either side. Lightly season with salt, remove and set aside. In the same casserole, sauté the finely chopped onions in two fresh tbsp. olive oil and add the garlic and ginger. Now add in the spice mix and stir well for 2 minutes to bring out the flavours.

Heat olive oil in a frying pan and quickly sauté the peeled, crushed tomatoes. Then add these tomatoes to the casserole with the onions and spices and add the amount of fish stock needed to cover everything. Cover the pot and simmer for 45 minutes, adding stock if needed.

Just before serving, add the fish steaks to the pot and allow to simmer for another 10–15 minutes depending on the fish texture. Season if needed. When it is ready, sprinkle with coriander leaves and serve with "grains" — basmati rice and lentils — not forgetting the bowl of tomato *chatini*.

Sharing the catch in a huge single dish

JUANITO'S *FIDEUA*

"This is a very old recipe that came from Valencia, and it is a fantastic one-course meal that is lovely to share with lots of people. Juanito, who is mostly in charge of desserts at the *Terrasses*, is also the master of *fideua*. He has reinterpreted the recipe in his Ibizan style, replacing the pigeon meat that is a bit strong-tasting by a *picada* of chicken livers that is much more subtle."

SERVES 10

Cooking time: 55 minutes +
15 minutes for the *picada* +
30 minutes for the fish stock

FOR THE *PICADA*

2 tomatoes
1 red pepper
2 cloves of garlic
2 chicken livers
1 bunch of parsley
Olive oil
Salt

FOR THE FISH STOCK

2 l (4 pints) fish stock, prepared using shop-bought dehydrated stock or home-made, with
1 kg (2 lb.) whitefish heads and bones (sea bream, sea bass, monkfish, sole, etc.)
1 onion
1 leek
1 carrot
1 celery stick
2 bay leaves
1 small sprig of rosemary
2 tbsp. olive oil
10 pepper grains
10 cl (6 tbsp.) dry white wine
2 l (4 pints) water

FOR THE GARNISH

500 g (1 lb.) shellfish
(clams or carpet shells)
300 g (10 oz.) large crab legs
(optional, and of course only
if you find them)
1 kg (2 lb.) prawns
2 chopped calamari
5 grouper steaks
2 chicken breasts
700 g (1½ lb.) large vermicelli
or shell pasta
1 tsp. saffron threads
Olive oil
Salt, pepper

First make the *picada*. Heat the olive oil in a frying pan over a hot flame and cook the chopped tomatoes and pepper, then the garlic in small cubes and the whole chicken livers. Salt lightly and cook for 15 minutes uncovered. At the end of this time, run everything through the food mixer, adding the parsley. Leave aside.

Prepare the fish stock, which must be hot when you use it. First heat the oil in a sauté pan over a low flame and add the whitefish heads and bones. Shake vigorously without browning. Add the sliced onion, carrot, leek and celery cut into large chunks, stir again and add the white wine, pepper, rosemary and bay leaf. Cover with 2 litres (4 pints) water and allow to simmer for 30 minutes uncovered. Then sieve.

Now put the shellfish into cold salted water to remove the sand. Rinse the large crab legs and the prawns. Clean the calamari and grouper steaks under the cold tap and cut into small pieces. Cut the chicken breasts into small pieces. Heat a little olive oil in a large frying pan over a hot flame and sauté the prawns for 3 minutes on either side. Reserve.

Now heat a little olive oil in a large wok or paella pan and fry the chicken, calamari and grouper pieces for about 10 minutes over a fairly hot flame. Then add the crab legs and the shellfish, stir and continue cooking for 5 minutes. Add the vermicelli, stir again. Add the *picada*, stir again and gradually pour in the hot fish stock. Season with the saffron, salt and pepper and simmer for about 20 minutes, stirring regularly, until the pasta has absorbed all the stock.

At the last minute, when the *fideua* seems cooked and virtually ready, add the prawns and leave the pan another three minutes over the heat. Serve piping hot!

"The frying pan is never big enough when all our friends turn up at the fishing cabin in the evening for a dish of *fideua*. So what we do is get it ready and simmer it slowly over a makeshift stove outside so that we can continue to admire the sunset over the sea. It's magical!"

ARROZ *A BANDA*

"This is a sort of paella with deliciously tasty rice, due to the tiny pieces of cuttlefish. I adore this one-serves-all dish — you put it in the middle of the table and everyone has a go with their forks. The best is at the end, when you scrape the brown bits at the bottom. The day we took the photos, Roshan had prepared it for us in a fisherman's cottage at Cala Salada."

SERVES 10

Preparation: make the stock
the day before
Cooking time: 4 hours 30 minutes
approx. including the stock

FOR THE STOCK

2 kg (4 lb.) fish (including rockfish)
3 sliced onions
2 celery sticks
4 finely chopped cloves of garlic
4 peeled tomatoes
I tsp. ground cinnamon
I tsp. mild pepper
2 bay leaves
I tbsp. pepper grains
2 carrots
I handful of chopped parsley

FOR THE *PICADA*

2 *noras* (small dried red peppers, not hot)
I fresh red pepper
4 whole tomatoes
6 tbsp. fresh, roasted almonds
I handful of parsley
½ tsp. saffron

FOR THE RICE

4 cuttlefish
2 tbsp. olive oil
2 cloves of garlic
I large onion
I kg (2 lb.) special paella rice
I glass of dry white wine
2 l (4 pints) previously prepared fish stock

First make the stock. Combine all the stock ingredients and simmer in 4 pints water for 3–4 hours over a medium flame. Then sieve.

Now prepare the *picada*. Cut all the vegetables into small pieces and fry in olive oil over a hot flame for 4–5 minutes in a frying pan. Meanwhile, peel the almonds and sauté them in I tbsp. olive oil over a medium flame for 5 minutes. Put the vegetables, almonds, parsley and saffron through the food mixer. Set aside.

Finally, prepare the rice. Cut the cuttlefish into small pieces. Heat the olive oil in a large paella pan and fry the sliced garlic and onion. Add the cuttlefish, then the rice, white wine and *picada*. Wait 3–4 minutes, then gradually add the fish stock. The rice must absorb the liquid and remain slightly crunchy. As soon as the rice is cooked, cover the pan and allow to swell for 10 minutes.

Serve the dish directly in the paella pan, placing it in the centre of the table so that everyone can help him- or herself with a fork.

My basics

Breads, pastries and biscuits

Sauces and coulis

BLACK OLIVE SHORTCRUST PASTRY

"I use this to add flavour to a tomato tart and make a pretty colour harmony!"

SERVES 8

Preparation: chill the pastry for 1 hour
Cooking time: 25 minutes

A tart tin about 30 cm (12 in.) in diameter

250 g (8 oz.) pitted olives
125 g (4 oz.) softened butter +
a lump to grease the tin
250 g (8 oz.) plain flour (T45 or T55)

Begin by whizzing the olives in the mixer, then add the softened butter. Mix well. Put the flour in a large bowl and scatter the olive-butter mixture over the top. Rub in quickly. Form into a ball, cover in cling film and refrigerate for about 1 hour.

When ready to use, return the dough to room temperature a little before rolling out using very little flour so that it stays black. Lightly grease the tin and line it with the pastry, making sure it goes over the edges and forms a roll to stop the pastry shrinking into the tin during cooking.

This pastry can be cooked blind for 25 minutes at 170°C (340°F) but also with a filling.

SWEET CRUST PASTRY

"I use this delicious pastry for my apricot, plum or fig and rhubarb tarts."

SERVES 8

Preparation: chill the pastry for 1 hour
Cooking time: 15–20 minutes

A tart tin 30 cm (12 in.) in diameter

250 g (8 oz.) plain flour (T45 or T55)
80 g (2½ oz.) caster sugar + 1 tbsp. to sprinkle
on the pastry
2 pinches of salt
160 g (5 oz.) butter + 1 lump to grease the tin
3 cl (2 tbsp.) water

In a bowl, combine the flour, sugar, salt and butter cut in pieces. Rub together until the mixture forms breadcrumbs. Add the water and mix the dough into a ball. Do not knead; otherwise it will become tough.

Flatten it out in the slightly greased tart tin and refrigerate for at least one hour without pricking it.

When ready to use the shell, sprinkle with a tbsp. sugar and bake for 15–20 minutes at 180°C (360°F).

SHORTCRUST PASTRY

"I use this pastry for my Swiss chard and olive tart and for my fig Tarte Tatin."

SERVES 8–10

Preparation: chill for at least 30 minutes
Cooking time: 20 minutes

A tart tin about 30 cm (12 in.) in diameter

300 g (10 oz.) plain flour (T45 or T55)
150 g (5 oz.) softened butter + 1 lump to grease the tin
5–6 cl (3–4 tbsp.) water
2 pinches of salt

Place the flour in a bowl or a food mixer, add the 2 pinches of salt, then the butter cut into bits. Rub in the fat (or run the mixer) to form breadcrumb consistency. Then add water and mix as quickly as possible to form a ball. This must be done very fast, because once water is added, the pastry must not be worked; otherwise it becomes tough.

Roll out immediately and line the lightly greased tin, forming a roll over the edges to avoid shrinkage during cooking. Once the pastry is in the tin, there is no rush. It should chill in the refrigerator for at least 30 minutes or even a day. You can cover with cling film if wished.

To use the pastry, remove from the fridge ahead of time and leave to return to room temperature.

This pastry shell can be baked blind for 20 minutes at 170°C (340°F) but also with a filling for quiches.

DONA'S SUGAR CRUST PASTRY

"A recipe for sweet pastry as good as shortbread, that Dona, a friend of my mother Henriette, gave to me. It makes lemon tart even better!"

SERVES 8 APPROX.

Preparation: chill for 1 hour
Cooking time: 15 minutes

For a tart tin 28 cm (10½ in.) in diameter

250 g (8 oz.) plain flour (T45 or T55)
125 g (4 oz.) softened butter
80 g (2½ oz.) caster sugar
1 pinch of salt
1 egg

Place the flour in a bowl and combine with the butter cut into bits that has been left at room temperature, the sugar and the pinch of salt. Lightly rub in until the mixture resembles breadcrumbs. Add the egg and gather together into a ball. Do not knead as it will become hard.

Personally, I flatten my pastry directly into the tin before chilling but you can also leave it in a ball and cover with cling film. In both cases, refrigerate for at least 1 hour.

When you roll out your pastry and line the tin, make sure you form a roll over the edges to prevent too much shrinkage during cooking.

Bake blind for 15 minutes at 170°C (340°F).

BRETON-STYLE
SHORTBREAD BISCUITS

"This is a *Terrasses* basic. We always serve a small round shortbread biscuit with coffee, and these sweet and salty biscuits are just delicious with all our sorbets or with peaches poached in verbena."

MAKES ABOUT 50 SMALL BISCUITS
Preparation: chill dough for 1 hour
Cooking time: 14 minutes

One or several silicone mini-muffin or bun trays

430 g (15 oz.) plain flour (T45 or T55)
4 g (scant tsp.) salt
250 g (8 oz.) caster sugar
2½ tsp. baking powder
300 g (10 oz.) softened butter
7 organic egg yolks

In a large mixing bowl, combine the flour, salt, sugar and baking powder, and add the butter cut into pieces. Rub it into the dry ingredients until it reaches breadcrumb consistency. Add the egg yolks, mix quickly and form a long sausage that has the same diameter as the cups in your mould. Cover with cling film and refrigerate for about 1 hour. This dough can be kept 3–4 days in the refrigerator but you can also freeze it. In this case, remember to take out your dough 30 minutes before baking.

When ready to bake your biscuits, remove the dough from the fridge, cut into slices that must not be thicker than half the depth of the cups in your mould and fill the tray.

Bake for 14 minutes at 180°C (360°F).

SMALL PITA BREADS

"Pita bread is the slightly thick flat bun usually eaten in southeastern Europe and the Middle East. I got the recipe from Ibán Yarza, a great bread maker who comes to give me classes at the Terrasses from time to time."

MAKES ABOUT TEN PITA
Preparation: prove the dough for 1 hour
Cooking time: 5 minutes

450 g (15 oz.) plain flour (T55)
50 g (1½ oz.) wholemeal flour
7 g (¼ oz.) fresh baker's yeast
(or 2.5 g [½ tsp.] dry yeast)
10 g (2 tsp.) salt
15 g (3 tsp.) caster sugar
25.5 cl (1 cup) water
1 tbsp. olive oil

In a bowl, combine the two flours, yeast, salt (make sure the salt does not touch the yeast — otherwise it will be killed), sugar, oil and water. Mix quickly using your hands and form a ball. Leave this to rise at room temperature or in the oven at 30°C (85°F) for 15 minutes. Knead the dough for 5 minutes on a floured board, folding it over several times. Then put it in a bowl and cover with cling film or a cloth, leaving it to rise again for 30 minutes at room temperature.

Preheat the oven to 250°C (480°F). Once the dough has risen, knead again and form balls of about 80–85g (2–3 oz.). Roll them in your hands, then flatten them with the rolling pin and make circles 15 cm (6 in.) in diameter. Lay on greaseproof paper and leave to rise again for 15 minutes under a slightly damp cloth.

To bake, slide the paper with the pita breads directly onto the hot oven tray. As soon as they begin to brown, turn them over. Count about 2 minutes per side for your pita breads to be perfectly cooked.

THE *TERRASSES* MERINGUES

"When we were on a cruise down the Nile, Adrian, the son of my friend Douce, spent his time preparing these meringues using the oven on the boat. That shows you it really is child's play and can be done anywhere! Old or young, everyone adores these at the *Terrasses*. They can always be found under a bell jar on the sitting-room table or on the old well like little welcoming gifts…"

MAKES ABOUT 60 SMALL MERINGUES
Cooking time: 1 hour 30 minutes

An icing pouch with a round fluted nozzle

6 egg whites
600 g (18 oz.) caster sugar
3 pinches of salt

Whip the egg whites and salt with an electrical whip. When they form peaks, add the sugar and beat for a very long time at medium speed, at least 10 minutes, until the texture is thick, very firm and a little silvery. Preheat the oven to 100°C (212°F).

Fill the icing pouch with the meringue mixture and drop small, evenly sized blobs (about 3 cm [1 in.] wide) in regular lines on greaseproof paper or silicone sheets spread over an oven tray.

Bake for an hour and a half. If your oven has a drying function, choose this at the start of cooking.

Remove from oven, allow to cool, then use a spatula to unstick the meringues and present them in a pretty cake dish.

AUBERGINE CAVIAR

"This is Oriane's recipe. It is particularly mild and I use it often for aperitifs or to enhance a few of my recipes like the grilled vegetable lasagne mille-feuille."

FOR A BOWL OF ABOUT 500 G (1 LB.)
Cooking time: 30 minutes

3 aubergines
2 small onions (or 1 large)
1 tbsp. tahini (sesame paste)
1 organic lemon
¼ tsp. salt
¼ tsp. pepper
Olive oil

Very gently grill the aubergines whole on a plancha or in a dry frying pan for a good 20 minutes, turning regularly with tongs. You can also bake them at 180–190°C (360–375°F) or grill them in a covered wok. Check the cooking until the flesh is soft inside. Allow to cool for about 15 minutes.

Sweat the sliced onions in a pan with a little olive oil over medium heat until they are transparent but not browned. Cut the aubergines in two and scrape out the flesh with a spoon.

In the mixer, combine the aubergine flesh, fried onions, tahini, lemon juice, salt and pepper and blend. Rectify the seasoning if needed with a drop of olive oil.

Refrigerate and serve cold on bread for aperitifs or as an ingredient in recipes.

JUANITO'S
TOMATO COULIS

"An essential ingredient in your pantry! You always need a little home-made coulis to enhance your dishes, vegetable terrines or even pasta. Use the tomato season in full summer to get in your supplies."

FOR TWO JARS, 385 ML (1.8 CUPS) EACH
Cooking time: 40 minutes approx.

2 onions
2 carrots
1 celery stick
1 kg (2 lb.) tomatoes
1 tsp. caster sugar
Olive oil
Salt, black pepper

Heat olive oil in a casserole and sweat the peeled, sliced onions with the carrots and celery cut into small pieces for 10 minutes over gentle heat. Add a little water if necessary.

Meanwhile, peel the tomatoes with a vegetable knife or by dropping them in boiling water for 20 seconds and then cut them into small pieces.

When the onions, carrots and celery are cooked, add in the tomatoes and cook for a good 15 minutes. Then add the sugar, salt and pepper. Continue to cook for a further 15 minutes approx.

When everything is cooked, put the sauce through the blender, then sieve.

Pour this coulis into carefully washed and dried jars. If you do not intend to use it immediately, sterilise the jars.

ROSHAN'S
CHILLI PASTE

"This is a basic in Indian cooking, and as a Mauritian cook, Roshan prepared it perfectly. At the *Terrasses*, we use it often to accompany ceviche, or Tahiti fish, or else oriental-style sea bream."

FOR A SMALL JAR, 50 CL (16 FL. OZ.)
No cooking

200 g (7 oz.) red bird's eye chillies
3 cloves of garlic
1 lime
2 tbsp. olive oil + a little for the jar
½ tsp. salt
1 tsp. black pepper

Remove the green stems of the chillies, preferably wearing gloves (chillies cause severe irritation). Peel the garlic and cut the unpeeled lime into pieces.

Combine the chillies, lime pieces, garlic and the two tbsp. olive oil in a food mixer with the salt and pepper. Blend.

Pour this paste into a jar, cover the surface with a centimetre of olive oil and close. Keep in the refrigerator.

You can use this paste immediately, but it keeps perfectly well for 3 months.

BLACK OLIVE
TAPENADE

"We use this as an aperitif spread on toast, as well as an accompaniment for grilled fish. Sometimes I replace the olives by sundried tomatoes in olive oil and it makes excellent tomato tapenade."

FOR ONE BOWL OF TAPENADE
No cooking

250 g (8 oz.) pitted black olives
10 anchovy fillets
1 tbsp. capers
3 drops of lemon juice
2 tbsp. olive oil
½ tsp. pepper

Combine all the ingredients — olives, anchovies, capers, lemon juice, olive oil and pepper. Blend, or better still, crush. That's it, you're done! Serve spread on toasted bread.

Tapenade can keep several days in the fridge.